COMPUTE!'s
Turbo C
for Beginners

Steve Burnap

COMPUTE! Publications,Inc.**abc**

A Capital Cities/ABC, Inc. Company
Greensboro, North Carolina

COMPUTE! Publications, Inc., Post Office Box 5406, Greensboro, NC 27403, (919) 275-9809, is a Capital Cities/ABC, Inc. Company and is not associated with any manufacturer of personal computers.

Turbo C is a trademark of Borland International Inc. IBM PC, PC XT, and PC AT are trademarks of International Business Machines Corporation.

Contents

Foreword

Turbo C is an amazing programming language. Its editor makes programming no more complex than writing a letter with a fully-featured word processor. And its compiler turns your program into machine language and executes it in a matter of seconds. And yet, because of the far-reaching power of *Turbo C*, its syntax and structure can be confusing and tortuous at first. Rather than give in to frustration, turn to *Turbo C for Beginners* from COMPUTE! Books, your friendly guide to this feature-packed language.

Author Steve Burnap has loaded his book with plenty of fully commented program examples and clear explanations written in everyday language. From your first *Turbo C* routines to the more complex programs later in the book, you'll progress with easy-to-follow steps.

After beginning with an explanation of compilers in Chapter 1, turn to Chapter 2 for your first guided tour of the features to be found in *Turbo C*. Chapter 3 explains the integrated programming environment, the system that turns your written words into machine language for the computer to execute.

In the chapters that follow, you'll learn advanced editing techniques as you build lesson upon lesson, until you fully understand the fundamentals of C. Chapter 9 is your guide to conditional statements, the instructions that simulate decision making. By the end of Chapter 11, you'll understand loops and how-to-build functions. In the final chapters, you'll put your new-found knowledge to work as you write a graphics routine, a simple database manager, and a poker-playing program.

Turbo C for Beginners is designed to grow with you. As your knowledge increases, so do the programming challenges posed. If you want to learn the fascinating language that is becoming an industry standard on the IBM PC, XT, AT and compatible personal computers, here is the book to get you started. By the time you're finished, you'll be a C programmer.

Acknowledgments

Thanks to Kris Land and the rest of the people at Paradox Corporation for the use of hardware, advice, and moral support.

Section One
An Introduction to *Turbo C*

Chapter 1

An Introduction to Compilers

If you're a beginning programmer, you may not yet know what a compiler actually does.

A compiler is a translation program. It translates a language that's fairly easy to understand into machine language, the only language a computer really understands.

In particular, the IBM PC understands a language called 8088 machine language. (ATs and PS/2s can also understand other languages like 80286 machine language and 80386 machine language.)

Machine Language

Machine language is meant only for machines. While it is possible for people to learn to read these programs, few would want to. Programs written in machine language usually consist of a series of binary numbers, which resembles random patterns of ones and zeros (Figure 1-1).

Figure 1-1. Raw Binary Machine Language

```
10101010101
11001011000
10100101101
11010101011
```

Each number represents a different instruction. To learn this language, you merely need to memorize hundreds of simple rules like those shown in Figure 1-2. Programming this way isn't really that complicated, just very, very tedious.

Figure 1-2. Rules of Machine Language

```
"Numbers    beginning    with    '101'    represent    'move'
instructions".
"Digits following a '101' represent the source and the
destination of the move".
```

In the early days of computing, a programmer had to learn machine language in order to write programs. When the machines were built, they only understood their own particular version of machine language. The only way programmers could communicate with them was through machine language.

Assemblers

This situation didn't last long, however. Programmers soon wrote special translation programs called assemblers. These programs read instructions written in a new language called assembly language and translated them into the corresponding machine language instructions. While assembly language is still not very easy to understand, it is far more readable than machine language. Figure 1-3 shows a few lines of assembly language instructions.

Figure 1-3. Assembly Language Example

```
MOV     R3,R2
INC     R2
ADD     R1,R3
CALL    SUB1
```

In assembly language, each word represents a single instruction. Because words are used rather than numbers, they are easier to understand and remember. The instruction 10111101 is difficult to comprehend. But it's fairly easy to understand the action of its assembly language equivalent, ADD.

As programs grew in size, they became increasingly difficult to write. Even simple tasks can require machine language programs that are many pages long. Theoretically, a 512K computer could hold thousands of pages of machine language instructions. Because each assembly language instruction represents a single machine language instruction, assembly language programs aren't any shorter than machine language programs. Assembly language programming can often become a battle as you wade through pages of printouts looking for a single erroneous instruction.

One of the reasons for long program listings is that assembly language instructions always deal with simple things, like storing values in registers. What was needed was a language that could be used at a higher level. Simple concepts such as printing a letter or drawing a circle could take hundreds of assembly language instructions. Programmers wanted a programming language in which a single statement could direct the machine to perform complex tasks.

Compilers
Soon, new languages called high-level languages were devised, and along with them came programs called compilers. A compiler takes a program written in a high-level language and converts it into a machine language program. High-level languages aren't as simple to understand as English, but they are easier to understand than machine or assembly language.

Turbo C
Turbo C is just such a compiler. It takes programs written in a high-level language called C and translates them into 8088 machine language.

Once you have read this book, programs like the one shown in Figure 1-4 will be fairly simple to read. With a fair amount of practice, you should be able to write simple C programs easily.

Figure 1-4. Simple C Program

```
#include   <stdio.h>

main()
{
   int total=0;
   int i;

   init_data();
   print_data();
}
```

C is just one of a number of different high-level languages. Other commonly used languages include Pascal, Fortran, BASIC, Cobol, Forth, Lisp, and Prolog. They all must be translated into machine language before being run.

Each language has different strengths and weaknesses. Just as with human languages, it is often easier to say certain things in different languages. Lisp is the language of artificial intelligence. You wouldn't want to use it to solve differential equations.

Each language has its own individual philosophy. This philosophy shapes both the structure of the language and the way it is used. COBOL, for instance, was created to be readable by nonprogrammers. Lisp was created to imitate certain areas of human thought. Prolog was created to use symbolic logic. These underlying philosophies dictate the strengths and weaknesses of each language.

C was created as a general-purpose language. Many languages have restrictions that force the programmer to write programs in a certain way. These restrictions make it easier to write programs for which the language was intended. But they make it hard to write other types of programs. The creators of C tried to put as few restrictions on the programmer as possible. This feature makes C a very powerful language, one useful in many different areas, but it also can make C difficult to use.

The popularity of C has grown tremendously over the past few years. It is quickly becoming the language of choice on the IBM PC and its compatibles. Many applications programmers like C because it allows them to access parts of the PC's architecture not available from other languages like Pascal or BASIC.

In order to protect the programmer from accidentally affecting certain parts of the machine, Pascal makes these areas very difficult to change. C allows you easy access to any part of the machine. This makes it easier for the programmer to use the machine to its full potential, but it also becomes easier to make mistakes that cause crashes.

Crashes

The previous paragraph might give a new programmer the impression that a single error in a C program could destroy the computer. This isn't the case. Unless you physically assault your computer, you aren't going to harm it.

Program code can cause the computer to cease functioning, however. This is a temporary state as described below. A program can fail in one of four ways, listed here in increasing severity:

• It does something you didn't intend. Your program will probably remain in memory.

- It ends prematurely, but leaves the computer in a normal state. Your program will probably remain in memory.
- It freezes the system. The machine will sit and do nothing. Repeated keypresses have no effect at first, but after a few keypresses, the computer begins to beep. This is a software crash. You'll have to press Ctrl-Alt-Del to restart the machine. If you didn't take the time to save your program before running it, it will be lost.
- It freezes the system. The machine doesn't respond to anything you do. Repeated keypresses have no effect. This is a hardware crash. You'll have to turn the machine off and then on again in order to restart the machine. Once again, if your program wasn't saved to disk, it will be lost.

Note that the worst crash you can cause using C can be repaired simply by turning the machine off and on again. People new to computers often fear that they may accidentally destroy the machine by using the wrong command. This cannot happen. You can accidentally destroy information stored in the machine, but the machine itself can only be destroyed through physical means. Note also that it is important to store your programs on disk before testing them. This procedure will help you to learn from your mistakes and save you a great deal of retyping.

The Origins of C

C didn't begin with the appearance of the PC. Its origins go back much farther.

C was created in the early seventies by AT&T for use on minicomputers. AT&T programmers liked the language so much that it soon spread to all AT&T machines. Eventually, C was used to create an operating system called Unix.

An operating system is a program that runs a computer. It allows the computer to interact with other devices such as disk drives and printers, and it helps the computer take care of its internal business, like interpreting the meaning of keypresses on the keyboard and placing letters and graphics on the monitor screen.

In the early 1980s, Unix spread to many business and college computers. The popularity of C spread along with it. C soon became the language of choice among many professional programmers.

Turbo C is a follow-up to Borland's very successful *Turbo Pascal* compiler. Because of its unique features and efficiency, *Turbo Pascal* has become the most successful Pascal compiler for the IBM PC. Borland has taken these features and added them to C, producing *Turbo C*. Many of these enhancements take advantage of the special features of the IBM PC.

Though this book will concentrate on *Turbo C*, an effort will be made to point out which features belong to *Turbo C* exclusively and which features are part of standard C. Changes made by Borland aren't changes to the structure of the C language. Rather, they are extensions created to use some of the special capabilities of the IBM personal computer. You should have little trouble using other versions of C on PCs or larger computers, once you have mastered *Turbo C*.

Chapter 2

A Short Tour Through
Turbo C

Turbo C operates differently from other versions of C editors
and compilers. Normally a compiler is called at the DOS
prompt and directed to translate a text file previously stored
on disk.

In order to write the text file, you must use a text editor
or word processor. Few compilers come with their own editors
so you're often stuck using a word processing program for
your editing. This isn't an ideal programming environment.
Because the editor and compiler are made by separate compa-
nies, they might not work well together. With this system, a
file must be saved to disk before being compiled.

The *Turbo C* Environment

The integrated *Turbo* C environment simplifies program writing and editing by combining the editor and compiler into a
single program.

To create a program, enter the *Turbo* C editor and type
the program text. When you have finished creating the program, you can run the *Turbo* C compiler directly from the
editor. You don't need to save the program to disk before
compiling it. You don't need to leave one program and load
another. Your program can be compiled with a single keystroke.

Because the file you are working on is held in memory instead of being stored on the disk before each compilation, the
integrated environment can translate programs much more
quickly than any conventional compiler.

Using a single program rather than a separate editor and
compiler has other benefits besides speed. The compiler can
send messages to the editor. If you make errors in your code
(and even highly trained, experienced programmers make errors), a conventional compiler would give you a list of errors
found in a program. You would have to write the errors down
on scratch paper and load the editor to find and fix the errors.

In the integrated *Turbo C* environment, however, the editor always knows about any errors found by the compiler. You don't need to keep track of them yourself. The *Turbo C* editor will show you exactly where each error was found by the compiler.

Sections of the Environment

The integrated *Turbo C* environment is divided into three parts.

- The editor is used to create or modify C programs in memory.
- The compiler is used to translate these programs into machine language.
- The filer moves these programs between the disk and memory.

Unlike most compilers, *Turbo C* translates programs from memory rather than from the disk. The file handler, accessed through the File menu, moves files between *Turbo C* and the disk. The filer is the only way *Turbo C* communicates with DOS (see Figure 2-1).

Figure 2-1. The Relationship of *Turbo C* and MS-DOS

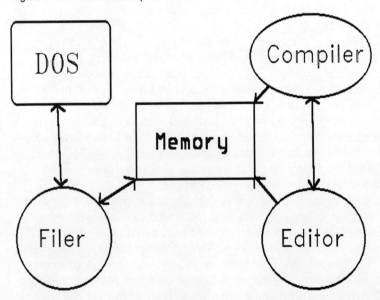

A programming session with a normal compiler (including the command-line *Turbo C* compiler discussed later in this book) might follow this pattern:

- Write program
- Save program
- Compile program
- Run program
- Load program
- Modify program
- Save program
- Compile program
- Run program

In *Turbo C*, you aren't required to save your program before you compile. Also, *Turbo C* will automatically compile your program for you whenever you run it. This reduces the number of commands that you have to remember. Using the integrated *Turbo C* environment, a typical session might look like this:

- Write program
- Run program
- Modify program
- Run program

Warnings

There is one subtle problem that a beginning programmer should be aware of. When using most other compilers, you're forced to save the file prior to compilation. You'll therefore have a current version of your program on disk each time you compile it. *Turbo C*, on the other hand, doesn't force you to do this. Programs are compiled directly from memory. You aren't required to use the disk at all. This means that you might not have a current version of the program on disk. Modifications and improvements can build up over hours of work, and a single momentary power failure can wipe out your work as thoroughly as if it had never been done. In order to prevent this loss, you should develop the habit of saving your work each time you make a major modification, just in case disaster strikes.

Turbo C does warn you if you're about to do something that could cause the loss of a program. For example, if you write or modify a program and then attempt to leave *Turbo C* without saving the file to disk, the window shown in Figure 2-2 will appear.

Figure 2-2. *Turbo C* Warns You to Save A Modified Program

```
     File      Edit      Run     Compile    Project    Options    Debug
╔═══════════════════════════════════════ Edit ═══════════════════════════╗
║      Load      F3 │1 2    Insert Indent Tab C:GAME.C                     ║
║ #in│ Pick   Alt-F3                                                       ║
║ #in│ New                                                                 ║
║ #in│ Save┌────────── Verify ──────────┐                                 ║
║ #in│ Writ│ GAME.C not saved.  Save? (Y/N)│                              ║
║ #in│ Dire└────────────────────────────┘                                 ║
║      Change dir                                                          ║
║      OS shell                                                            ║
║ #de│ Quit   Alt-X                                                        ║
║ #de                                                                      ║
║ #define RED 0x70                                                         ║
║ #define BLUE 0x71                                                        ║
║                                                                          ║
║ void *print_ships(ship *ship_list,scr screen):                          ║
╠══════════════════════════════════ Message ══════════════════════════════╣
║                                                                          ║
║                                                                          ║
║                                                                          ║
║                                                                          ║
╚══════════════════════════════════════════════════════════════════════════╝
  F1-Help   Esc-Abort
```

This window tells you that you're about to lose a modified file and asks you to confirm that this is what you want to do. Depending on your response to this prompt, you may save the file to the disk, or if you really want to throw it out, you may abandon it, leaving the original (if there was one) unchanged on disk. This helps protect you from the accidental loss of your program file.

Turbo C was written to ease the pain of programming. You should never be afraid to experiment. Short of a power failure, it is nearly impossible to accidently lose your work.

The Menu System

Turbo C uses a modified menu system. Menus are often used in programs because they are very easy to use, especially for the beginner. A menu always shows you exactly what you can do. You don't have to search through manuals to determine your options.

In *Turbo C*, for example, it's easy to save a file. First, look at the main menu and choose the File option. This brings up another menu. Looking at this menu, you'll see a Save option. Choose this option, and the file will be saved. Because you're using menus, there are no commands to remember. You just read the menu.

There is a disadvantage to menus, however. If you have used the system for months, it becomes tedious to wade through two or more menus just to execute a simple command. *Turbo C* provides shortcuts through its menu structure in the form of certain key commands. For example, in order to save a file, you may simply press the F2 key, no matter where you are in the *Turbo C* menu system. You don't need to wade through menus every time you want to save a file.

Turbo C provides the best of both worlds. The menu structure is friendly. The novice programmer will have little trouble finding his or her way around. On the other hand, powerful commands exist for the advanced programmer. You'll never feel bogged down by the friendly features. Power users and beginners both will find that *Turbo C* is designed to meet their needs.

Summary

This chapter has provided a brief explanation of the features of the *Turbo C* programming environment. As you advance in knowledge, you'll discover many shortcuts, either through reviewing this text or the *Turbo C* manuals. Don't attempt to learn everything at a single sitting. At first, it's enough to know how to use the menus to access the most fundamental commands. Later, when you have gained more confidence, you'll start to use some of the more advanced menu options. Don't feel pressured to learn everything. If you understand the menu system, you know enough to write most programs. You'll find that once you have learned the basics, the rest will fall into place.

Chapter 3
The Integrated Environment

This chapter will give you a short tour through the integrated *Turbo C* environment. You will learn to use the editor to create a short program which will then be converted to machine language using the compiler.

Installation

Before you can use *Turbo C*, it must be properly installed on your fixed disk. Please see the *Turbo C User's Guide* for installation instructions.

To start *Turbo C*, change to the *Turbo C* directory, type *tc*, and press Enter.

The screen will clear and you will see the *Turbo C* Edit window. In the middle of screen, you will see the *Turbo C* copyright notice (see Figure 3-1).

At the top of this screen is the main menu. There are seven different options on the main menu. If you have a color system, the File option will be colored purple. Otherwise, it will be highlighted. This highlighted bar allows you to select one of the options. Try pressing the → key. The copyright notice will disappear, and the highlighting will move to the Edit option. To select the File option, use the left or right cursor key to highlight it and press the Enter key. A pull-down menu will appear (Figure 3-2).

These menu options allow you to transfer files between disk and memory. The first option in this menu will be highlighted. You may use the up and down cursor keys to highlight any of the options on this menu. Pressing Enter will select the option that you have highlighted.

Figure 3-1. The *Turbo C* Copyright Notice

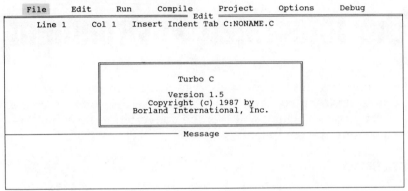

File	Edit	Run	Compile	Project	Options	Debug

══════════════════════════════ Edit ══════════════════════════════
Line 1   Col 1   Insert Indent Tab C:NONAME.C

```
                    Turbo C

                   Version 1.5
              Copyright (c) 1987 by
              Borland International, Inc.
```

─────────────────── Message ───────────────────

F1-Help F5-Zoom F6-Edit F9-Make F10-Main Menu

Figure 3-2. The File Menu

File	Edit	Run	Compile	Project	Options	Debug

══════════════════════════════ Edit ══════════════════════════════
```
Load      F3   1 1   Insert Indent Tab C:NONAME.C
Pick  Alt-F3
New
Save      F2
Write to
Directory
Change dir
OS shell
Quit    Alt-X
```

─────────────────── Message ───────────────────

F1-Help F5-Zoom F6-Edit F9-Make F10-Main Menu

The Edit Window

When you begin work on a program, you need to tell *Turbo C*
that you want a new program. Move the cursor to the word
New and press Enter. The menu will disappear, and you will
see a flashing underscore in the Edit window (Figure 3-3).

Figure 3-3. The Flashing Underscore in the Edit Window

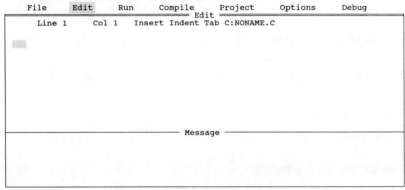

The flashing underscore is the text cursor. You are now in the editor portion of *Turbo C.* Start typing. The words you type will appear in the Edit window (Figure 3-4).

Figure 3-4. Typing in the Edit Window

```
    File      Edit      Run     Compile     Project     Options     Debug
═══════════════════════════════════ Edit ═══════════════════════════════════
     Line 1      Col 23    Insert Indent Tab C:NONAME.C
This is a test of the░░░



                               ───── Message ─────



═════════════════════════════════════════════════════════════════════════════
 F1-Help  F5-Zoom  F6-Message  F9-Make  F10-Main menu
```

At the top of the edit window is the editor status line. The status line provides information about the editor. At the left end of the status line you will see something like

line 1 col 23

This refers to the position of the cursor within the text. The word *line* refers to the line that the cursor is currently on.

17

In this case, the cursor is on the first line. The word *col* describes the column position of the cursor within that line. In this case, the cursor is on the twenty-third column in the first line.

The only other section of the status line important to you at this time is the current filename, which is shown at the right end of the status line. Because you haven't named your file, this should say

C:\TURBOC\NONAME.C

Later, when you save your file, you will give it a name.

Leaving the Edit Window

To save your file, go back to the File menu. You must first go to the main menu to do this. How do you get to the main menu? Look at the bottom of the screen. *Turbo C* will always list important function keys and their use here. From the editor, the F10 key will take you to the main menu.

Press F10, move the cursor to the File option, and press Enter. This will cause the file options to appear again. From this menu, choose the Save option. A small window will appear (Figure 3-5).

Figure 3-5. Window Requesting Filename

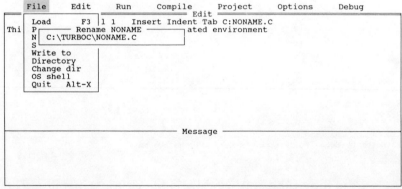

Currently your filename is NONAME.C. *Turbo C* recognizes that this isn't the name you chose for the file, and it will ask you to make up a new name. The window contains space in which you can enter a new name. If you press Enter at this time, the file will be saved with the name NONAME.C. To choose a different name, simply type one in. As you press the first key, the old name (NONAME.C) will disappear. You can then replace it with a name of your choosing. For the purpose of this demonstration, type in *myfirst.c* and press Enter (see Figure 3-6).

Figure 3-6. Enter New Name

```
   File     Edit     Run     Compile    Project    Options    Debug
                                    Edit
       Load      F3 |1 1   Insert Indent Tab C:NONAME.C
 Thi   P  ┌──── Rename NONAME ──────┐ated environment
       N  │ myfirst.c               │
       S  └────────────────────────┘
       Write to
       Directory
       Change dir
       OS shell
       Quit    Alt-X




                         ── Message ──



```

F1-Help Esc-Abort

Turbo C will save the file, and you'll be returned to the File menu. To check whether your file was saved, choose the directory option. Another small window will appear, as in Figure 3-7, requesting a directory mask.

What is a mask? A mask allows you to specify a pattern for the filename you are looking for. This will be explained in detail momentarily. If you have many files, a directory mask will reduce the list you have to look at. Currently, there probably aren't enough files to bother with a mask. Just press Enter.

Figure 3-7. Directory Mask

```
   File      Edit      Run    Compile     Project     Options     Debug
════════════════════════════════════ Edit ═══════════════════════════════
   ┌──────────────┐ 1 54  Insert Indent Tab C:MYFIRST.C
   │ Load     F3  │ he Turbo C Integrated environment
Thi│ Pick  Alt-F3 │
   │ New          │
   │ Save     F2  │
   │ Write to     │
   │ Directory    │
   │  ┌─── Enter Mask ───┐
   │  │ *.*              │
   └──┤                  │
      └──────────────────┘

                         ─── Message ───

────────────────────────────────────────────────────────────────────────
F1-Help  Esc-Abort
```

A larger window will appear containing a list of all your files as shown in Figure 3-8. In this list of files, you should see one called MYFIRST.C, which means that your file has been saved to disk.

Figure 3-8. Directory Window

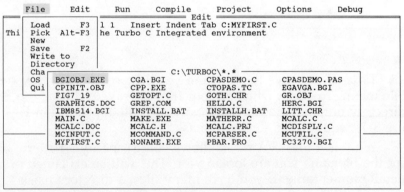

```
   File      Edit      Run    Compile     Project     Options     Debug
════════════════════════════════════ Edit ═══════════════════════════════
   ┌──────────────┐ 1 1   Insert Indent Tab C:MYFIRST.C
   │ Load     F3  │ he Turbo C Integrated environment
Thi│ Pick  Alt-F3 │
   │ New          │
   │ Save     F2  │
   │ Write to     │
   │ Directory    │
   │ Cha          ──────── C:\TURBOC\*.* ─────────────────────────────┐
   │ OS  │ BGIOBJ.EXE    CGA.BGI        CPASDEMO.C     CPASDEMO.PAS    │
   │ Qui │ CPINIT.OBJ    CPP.EXE        CTOPAS.TC      EGAVGA.BGI      │
   └─────│ FIG7_19       GETOPT.C       GOTH.CHR       GR.OBJ          │
         │ GRAPHICS.DOC  GREP.COM       HELLO.C        HERC.BGI        │
         │ IBM8514.BGI   INSTALL.BAT    INSTALLH.BAT   LITT.CHR        │
         │ MAIN.C        MAKE.EXE       MATHERR.C      MCALC.C         │
         │ MCALC.DOC     MCALC.H        MCALC.PRJ      MCDISPLY.C      │
         │ MCINPUT.C     MCOMMAND.C     MCPARSER.C     MCUTIL.C        │
         │ MYFIRST.C     NONAME.EXE     PBAR.PRO       PC3270.BGI      │
         └──────────────────────────────────────────────────────────────┘

────────────────────────────────────────────────────────────────────────
F1-Help  F4-New mask  ↑↓→hoose  <─┘-Select  Esc-Abort
```

The Search Mask

When you use the directory option to look at the disk, the search mask is compared with each file. Filenames that match the mask are displayed, but others are not. In the previous example, *.* was the search mask. An asterisk in a search mask will match any character or sequence of characters. The above mask will show you any file that contains a period.

You will often want to use another mask. The mask *.C will tell *Turbo C* to show you only files ending with a .C extension. Because all C program files normally end with a .C, this mask can be used to show your C programs without cluttering the screen with other files. Choose the directory option again and enter

*.C

when it asks for a mask. This listing will probably only show the file you entered earlier, MYFIRST.C (Figure 3-9).

Figure 3-9. Directory with *.C Mask

```
     File      Edit      Run     Compile    Project    Options    Debug
┌────────────────────────────────────── Edit ═══════════════════════════════
│     Load      F3  │1 1    Insert Indent Tab C:MYFIRST.C
│Thi│ Pick   Alt-F3 │he Turbo C Integrated environment
│   │ New            │
│   │ Save     F2    │
│   │ Write to       │
│   │ Directory      │
│   │ Cha┌────────────────────── C:\TURBOC\*.C ──────────────────────┐
│   │ OS │ BAR.C          BGIDEMO.C       CPASDEMO.C      GETOPT.C    │
│   └─── HELLO.C         MAIN.C          MATHERR.C       MCALC.C     │
│       │ MCDISPLY.C      MCINPUT.C       MCOMMAND.C      MCPARSER.C  │
│       │ MCUTIL.C        MYFIRST.C       INCLUDE\        LIB\        │
│       │ PROGS\          ..\                                         │
│       │                                                            │
│       │                                                            │
│       └────────────────────────────────────────────────────────────┘
│
└────────────────────────────────────────────────────────────────────
  F1-Help  F4-New mask  ↑↓→hoose   <─┘-Select  Esc-Abort
```

Now select the Quit option. The screen will clear, and you will be placed at the DOS prompt. Enter the word

DIR

and press Enter. Among the files listed should be MYFIRST.C (Figure 3-10).

Figure 3-10. DOS Directory

```
C:\TURBOC>dir *.c

 Volume in drive C is COMPUTE!
 Directory of  C:\TURBOC

HELLO     C        110  11-19-87   1:05a
CPASDEMO  C       1682  11-19-87   1:05a
BAR       C       3878  11-19-87   1:05a
MAIN      C       1102  11-19-87   1:05a
MCALC     C       3616  11-19-87   1:05a
MCINPUT   C       4220  11-19-87   1:05a
MCOMMAND  C      18973  11-19-87   1:05a
MCPARSER  C      12225  11-19-87   1:05a
MCUTIL    C      15086  11-19-87   1:05a
MCDISPLY  C       6690  11-19-87   1:05a
BGIDEMO   C      42530  11-19-87   1:05a
MATHERR   C       3850  11-19-87   1:05a
GETOPT    C       4228  11-19-87   1:05a
MYFIRST   C         59   1-06-88  10:46a
        14 File(s)    2107392 bytes free

C:\TURBOC>
```

Now return to *Turbo C* by typing

tc

and pressing Enter. Select the Edit option on the main menu.
You can see that anything you typed earlier is gone. When-
ever you leave *Turbo C*, any file in memory will be discarded.
But since you took the time to save the file to disk, it isn't lost.
You can retrieve it using the Load option on the File menu.
menu.

Press F10 to return to the main menu, and select File. Select the Load option. Another small window will appear (Figure 3-11).

This window closely resembles the search-mask window
you saw earlier. In this case, *.C is the mask. As you know,
this mask will show only C programs. Press Enter to accept
this mask. A new directory window will appear (See Figure
3-12).

Figure 3-11. Load Filename Window

```
  File       Edit      Run      Compile     Project     Options     Debug
┌──────────────────────────────── Edit ═══════════════════════════════
│ Load      F3 │1 1    Insert Indent Tab  C:NONAME.C
│┌─── Load File Name ────────────┐
││ *.C                           │
│└───────────────────────────────┘
│ Write to
│ Directory
│ Change dir
│ OS shell
│ Quit   Alt-X
└─────────────┘
                        ───────────── Message ──────────────────
```

F1-Help Esc-Abort

Figure 3-12. The Load Directory Window

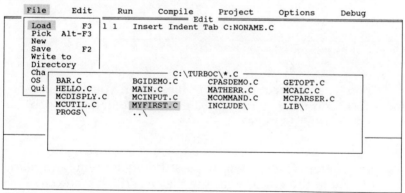

```
  File       Edit      Run      Compile     Project     Options     Debug
┌──────────────────────────────── Edit ═══════════════════════════════
│ Load      F3 │1 1    Insert Indent Tab  C:NONAME.C
│ Pick  Alt-F3
│ New
│ Save      F2
│ Write to
│ Directory
│ Cha┌─────────────────── C:\TURBOC\*.C ───────────────────┐
│ OS │ BAR.C       BGIDEMO.C    CPASDEMO.C    GETOPT.C      │
│ Qui│ HELLO.C     MAIN.C       MATHERR.C     MCALC.C       │
│    │ MCDISPLY.C  MCINPUT.C    MCOMMAND.C    MCPARSER.C    │
│    │ MCUTIL.C    MYFIRST.C    INCLUDE\      LIB\          │
│    │ PROGS\      ..\                                      │
│    └──────────────────────────────────────────────────────┘
```

F1-Help F4-New mask ↑↓→hoose <─┘-Select Esc-Abort

You may use the four cursor keys to move the highlighted bar among the files. To load a file, move the cursor to its name and press Enter. Load MYFIRST.C. *Turbo C* will load the file and place you in the editor (Figure 3-13). Notice that the filename on the status line is now MYFIRST.C instead of NONAME.C.

Figure 3-13. The File Loads, and Control Is Transferred to Edit Window

```
   File   Edit    Run    Compile    Project   Options   Debug
================================ Edit ===============================
    Line 1      Col 1    Insert Indent Tab C:MYFIRST.C
 This is a test of the Turbo C Integrated environment




                        ───── Message ─────



 F1-Help  F5-Zoom  F6-Message  F9-Make  F10-Main menu
```

There is a shortcut to loading files when you first run *Turbo C*. If you want to run *Turbo C* and automatically load the file MYFIRST.C, type

tc myfirst.c

and press Enter. *Turbo C* will bypass the main menu and place you directly in the editor with the file MYFIRST.C automatically loaded.

More on Saving

Make some changes to your file as shown in Figure 3-14.

If you were to leave *Turbo C* now, your changes would be lost, so save these changes to the disk. Use F10 to go to the main menu, enter the File menu and select the Save option.

The word *Saving . . .* will flash across the bottom of your screen. Your file is saved. Why didn't it ask for a filename? When you had previously saved this file, you gave it the name MYFIRST.C. Once you have named a file, *Turbo C* will assume that you will want to use this name whenever you save the file.

24

Figure 3-14. A Changed File

```
     File    Edit     Run     Compile     Project     Options     Debug
                               Edit
    Line 5       Col 1   Insert Indent Tab C:MYFIRST.C
This is a test of the Turbo C Integrated environment


Here are some changes






                              Message




```

F1-Help F5-Zoom F6-Edit F9-Make F10-Main Menu

How do you know what name *Turbo C* will use? *Turbo C* always uses the name that appears on the status line in the editor. If this is NONAME.C, *Turbo C* will assume that it is a new file and will ask you for a new name. Otherwise it will use the filename you gave when you loaded the file or saved it last.

Suppose you make some changes and want to save them to a new file? What then? Make some changes to the current file now (Figure 3-15).

Figure 3-15. File with Additional Changes

```
     File    Edit     Run     Compile     Project     Options     Debug
                               Edit
    Line 5       Col 27  Insert Indent Tab C:MYFIRST.C
This is a test of the Turbo C Integrated environment


Here are some changes

Here are some more changes





                              Message




```

F1-Help F5-Zoom F6-Message F9-Make F10-Main menu

Now go into the File menu. Select the Write to option. This will cause a small window labeled New Name to appear. Enter the words *mysecond.c* in this window as in Figure 3-16.

Figure 3-16. New File Window

```
    File     Edit     Run    Compile   Project    Options    Debug
                                  Edit
 ┌─────────────────────┬───────────────────────────────────────┐
 │   Load      F3      │ 1 27   Insert Indent Tab C:MYFIRST.C   │
 │Thi│ Pick   Alt-F3   │ he Turbo C Integrated environment      │
 │   New               │
 │   Save      F2      │
 │Her│ Write to    │   es
 │       New Name
 │Her│ mysecond.c              │
 │
 │   Quit    Alt-X │
 │
 │
 │
 │                          Message
 │
 │
 │
 └────────────────────────────────────────────────────────────┘
 F1-Help   Esc-Abort
```

Now press Enter. *Turbo C* will save the file with the new name. Now use the right cursor key to highlight the Edit option and press Enter. Look at the status line. Notice that the filename in the status line is now MYSECOND.C rather than MYFIRST.C. If you were to select the Save option again, *Turbo C* would use the name MYSECOND.C.

Compiling

Now you are ready to actually compile and run a program. Enter the File menu and select the New option. This will place you in the editor. Now enter the text shown in Figure 3-17.

Make sure that the text on your screen matches the text in the figure. What do you do if you make a mistake? The backspace key will erase the character to the left of the cursor. You may remove more characters by repeatedly pressing the backspace key.

If you discover a mistake in the middle of a file, you can fix it by using the cursor keys to move through the file. By moving the cursor directly after erroneous characters and using backspace key, you can remove unwanted characters from a file. If you need to add characters in the middle, simply use the cursor keys to move to the correct position and type in

Figure 3-17. Your First C Program

```
     File      Edit      Run      Compile    Project      Options      Debug
═══════════════════════════════════════ Edit ═══════════════════════════════════
     Line 6      Col 53   Insert Indent Tab C:NONAME.C
#include <stdio.h>

main()
{
     printf("Hello, this is my first C program\n")
     printf("written in the integrated environment");




─────────────────────────────── Message ────────────────────────────────────




```
F1-Help F5-Zoom F6-Message F9-Make F10-Main menu

the letters. Any characters already there will be moved to make way for the new characters.

Once you have satisfied yourself that your program matches the example in Figure 3-17, you can run the program. Go to the main menu and select the Run option. A new window will suddenly appear on the screen (Figure 3-18).

Figure 3-18. Compiling Window

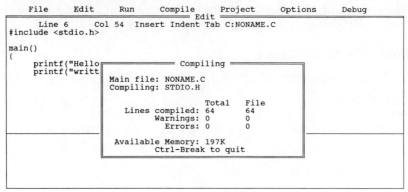

```
     File      Edit      Run      Compile    Project      Options      Debug
═══════════════════════════════════════ Edit ═══════════════════════════════════
     Line 6      Col 54   Insert Indent Tab C:NONAME.C
#include <stdio.h>

main()
{
     printf("Hello┌──────────── Compiling ═══════════┐
     printf("writt│                                  │
                  │ Main file: NONAME.C              │
                  │ Compiling: STDIO.H               │
                  │                  Total    File   │
                  │ Lines compiled:  64       64     │
                  │       Warnings:  0        0      │
                  │         Errors:  0        0      │
                  │                                  │
                  │ Available Memory: 197K           │
                  │      Ctrl-Break to quit          │
                  └──────────────────────────────────┘



```
F1-Help F5-Zoom F6-Edit F7/F8-Prev/Next error F9-Make F10-Main Menu

Turbo C will compile your program into machine language. Soon, one of two things will happen: Either *Turbo C* will understand the program and run it, or it will report an error.

The program you typed in contains an error. This was done intentionally to show how *Turbo C* handles errors. The message shown in Figure 3-19 should appear.

Figure 3-19. Error Message

```
   File     Edit     Run    Compile    Project    Options    Debug
                          ════════ Edit ════════
   ┌──────────────────────────────────────────────────────────────┐
   │  Line 6     Col 54   Insert Indent Tab C:NONAME.C             │
   │#include <stdio.h>                                              │
   │                                                                │
   │main()                                                          │
   │{                                                               │
   │    printf("Hello┌═══════════ Compiling ═══════════┐           │
   │    printf("writt│                                  │           │
   │                 │ Main file: NONAME.C              │           │
   │                 │ Compiling: EDITOR → NONAME.C     │           │
   │                 │                                  │           │
   │                 │                    Total   File  │           │
   │                 │  Lines compiled: 215     215     │           │
   │                 │       Warnings: 0         0      │           │
   │                 │         Errors: 2         2      │           │
   │                 │                                  │           │
   │                 │ Available Memory: 204K           │           │
   │                 │ Errors          :    Press any key│          │
   │                 └══════════════════════════════════┘          │
   │                                                                │
   └──────────────────────────────────────────────────────────────┘
   F1-Help  F5-Zoom  F6-Edit  F7/F8-Prev/Next error  F9-Make  F10-Main Menu
```

Press the space bar. The compiling window will disappear. You have probably already noticed the message window that fills the bottom third of the screen. It should now be filled with a number of messages. This is a list of the things that *Turbo C* couldn't understand about your program. The first of these will be covered with a highlighted bar (Figure 3-20).

Figure 3-20. Error Messages

```
   File     Edit     Run    Compile    Project    Options    Debug
                          ════════ Edit ════════
   ┌──────────────────────────────────────────────────────────────┐
   │  Line 6     Col 12   Insert Indent Tab C:NONAME.C             │
   │#include <stdio.h>                                              │
   │                                                                │
   │main()                                                          │
   │{                                                               │
   │    printf("Hello, this is my first C program\n")              │
   │    printf("written in the integrated environment");           │
   │                                                                │
   │                                                                │
   │                          ════ Message ════                     │
   │Compiling C:\TURBOC\NONAME.C:                                   │
   │Error C:\TURBOC\NONAME.C 6: Statement missing ; in function main│
   │Error C:\TURBOC\NONAME.C 7: Compound statement missing } in function main│
   └──────────────────────────────────────────────────────────────┘
   F1-Help  F5-Zoom  F6-Edit  F7/F8-Prev/Next error  F9-Make  F10-Main Menu
```

Turbo C will show you exactly where each error occurred. Look at the bottom of the screen. You will notice the words

F6 Edit

You may enter the editor by pressing the F6 key (Figure 3-21). The cursor will be placed at the first error.

Figure 3-21. Note Position of Cursor in Edit Window

```
    File      Edit      Run     Compile     Project     Options     Debug
                            ──────── Edit ────────
    Line 7       Col 1    Insert Indent Tab C:NONAME.C
#include <stdio.h>

main()
{
    printf("Hello, this is my first C program\n")
    printf("written in the integrated environment");



                            ═══════ Message ═══════
Compiling C:\TURBOC\NONAME.C:
Error C:\TURBOC\NONAME.C 6: Statement missing ; in function main
Error C:\TURBOC\NONAME.C 7: Compound statement missing } in function main


```

F1-Help F5-Zoom F6-Edit F7/F8-Prev/Next error F9-Make F10-Main Menu

Press F8. That will move the cursor to the second error. The second message in the message window will be highlighted.

Press F8 again. That will show you the third message.

Press F7. That will bring you back to the second error. Using these two keys you can quickly find all of the errors in your program.

At this point, don't worry about the messages themselves. The correct version of the program is shown in Figure 3-22.

Change your program so that it matches Figure 3-22. You can easily spot the differences by using the F7 and F8 keys.

Once the changes have been made, run the program again by selecting the Run option from the main menu. If all of the changes have been made correctly, the screen will clear, and your program will print a friendly message on the screen (Figure 3-23).

Figure 3-22. Corrected Version of C Program

```
     File      Edit     Run     Compile     Project     Options     Debug
                                 = Edit =
      Line 1      Col 1     Insert Indent Tab C:NONAME.C
 #include <stdio.h>

 main()
 {
      printf("Hello, this is my first C program\n");
      printf("written in the integrated environment");
 }




                                 Message
 Compiling C:\TURBOC\NONAME.C:
 Error C:\TURBOC\NONAME.C 6: Statement missing ; in function main


```

F1-Help F5-Zoom F6-Message F7/F8-Prev/Next error F9-Make F10-Main Menu

Figure 3-23. The Result of Program

```
Hello, this is my first C program
Written in the integrated environment
```

```
Press any key to return to Turbo C . . .
```

You have successfully written and run your first program in C. That's probably enough for one chapter. Go to the File menu and choose the Quit option (Figure 3-24).

Figure 3-24. Prompt to Save Altered Program Before Exiting

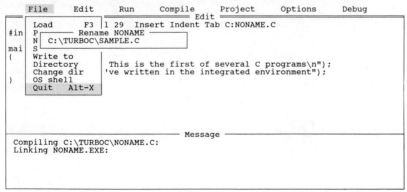

What happened? You were about to leave the editor without saving your file. You would have lost it if *Turbo C* had let you do this. *Turbo C* keeps track of whether the file in memory has been saved. If you try to exit without saving, *Turbo C* will ask you whether it should save the file. If you were to type *N* now, all of your changes would be lost. You probably don't want to do this. Type *Y*. This will automatically perform a save command (Figure 3-25).

Figure 3-25. Prompt to Save NONAME.C Program Under a New Name

```
    File      Edit      Run     Compile    Project    Options    Debug
 ═══════════════════════════════════════ Edit ════════════════════════════
     Load      F3 |1 29   Insert Indent Tab C:NONAME.C
#in  P┌─────── Rename NONAME ──────┐
     N│ C:\TURBOC\SAMPLE.C         │
mai  S└────────────────────────────┘
(    Write to
     Directory      This is the first of several C programs\n");
     Change dir    've written in the integrated environment");
}    OS shell
     Quit   Alt-X
 ──────────────────────────────────── Message ──────────────────────────
  Compiling C:\TURBOC\NONAME.C:
  Linking NONAME.EXE:

 F1-Help  Esc-Abort
```

31

Because you haven't yet named the program, *Turbo C* asks you for a new name. If the file had already had a name other than NONAME.C, then it wouldn't have prompted you for a name. Once the file is saved, you will exit *Turbo C* and return to DOS.

Summary

During the course of this chapter, you have learned how to install *Turbo C*, how to work with files, and how to use the Edit window. You learned how to compile *Turbo C* programs into executable code and how to deal with error messages. This is the most basic information on programming with the *Turbo C* package. If there are any points you aren't sure about, reread the section in this chapter and consult your owner's manual. You will need this information as you progress in this book.

Chapter 4
C Program Structure

This chapter will give a brief overview of how C programs are put together. The terms presented here will give you a basic understanding of the structures used in the construction of C programs.

Statements

All C programs are made up of a sequence of statements. A statement can generally be thought of as a single action. A statement in C is much like a sentence in English. Both consist of a sequence of words (commands) terminated by a single character. (Sentences in English are ended with periods. Statements in C are ended with semicolons.) Figure 4-1 contains some example C statements.

Figure 4-1. Some C Statements

```
int i;

a = a+1;

while(z<23) a = a + 54;
```

It's usually considered good form to avoid using more than one statement on a single line. If you start each statement on a new line, it will be easier to distinguish between statements. This is not a requirement of the compiler, but you'll appreciate this convention if you return to your code to make revisions. Writing code that is clear and easily read is like giving yourself a gift. Six months from now the exact program flow may be fuzzy in your memory, if any memory of it remains at all. If you write your code clearly, you'll be able to read and comprehend it instantly when you return to it.

Statements generally fall into two categories.

- Executable
- Declarative

Executable statements contain commands that perform actions. Such statements must be placed inside a block (located between a pair of curly braces).

Declarative statements set up structures the program needs to operate. (Structures will be explained in greater detail later on.) Declarative statements may occur inside or outside of a block, but if they are inside a block, they must come first, before any executable statements. Declarative statements create the environment for the executable statements that follow.

The following special declaration statement must occur in every C program:

main( )

This statement identifies where the program will begin executing. This declaration statement will always be followed by a single block (which may, in turn, contain other blocks) that contains the executable statements for your program.

Blocks

Statements are grouped together in units called blocks. A block can be any group of statements and other blocks. Braces ({ }) are used to mark the beginning and ending of a block. Figure 4-2 shows some examples of blocks.

Figure 4-2. Blocks Set Apart by Braces

```
z = z * x;                          /* block 1 */

{                                   /* block 2 */
    print_it();
    for(i=10;i<100;i++)
        get_it();
}

{                                   /* block 3 */
    {                               /* block 3-a */
        {                           /* block 3-b */
            int i = 456;
            i=i+31;
            printf("%d",i);
        }
        print_number(j);
    }
}
```

Notice the formatting of the block. Each brace is placed alone on a line. Statements inside the braces are indented slightly. This helps the programmer distinguish more easily between blocks. This is not a requirement of the compiler, but it is good programming practice.

Compiler Directives

In addition to statements and blocks, a C program may also contain commands to the compiler. These commands (called compiler directives) are not part of the actual program itself. Instead, these commands direct the translation of the other statements in the program. These commands will always begin with the pound symbol (#). They may occur anywhere in the file, but unlike other commands, compiler directives must appear alone on a single line.

Comments

Finally, programs may also contain comments. A comment is not a command and has absolutely no effect on program execution. The sole purpose of a comment is to help explain the operation of the program to any programmer who looks at the program code. Since you're the programmer most likely to be going over the code, remember that code with many comments is much easier to understand at a glance. Putting comments in your code is another gift you can give yourself.

Comments must begin with the characters /* and end with the characters */.

/* Your comment here */

A comment can occur nearly anywhere in a program, even in the middle of another command. The sole exception to this rule is that comments should not be placed inside other comments. You can instruct *Turbo C* to allow nested comments, but this is not a standard feature of C and should be avoided.

A C Program

In summary, a C program will usually have a structure similar to that shown in Figure 4-3.

Figure 4-3. A Sample C Program

```
#compiler directive1
#compiler directive2          /* Comment */

declaration1;                 /* Another comment */
declaration2;

main()
{
     declaration3;            /* Declarations can occur in blocks
*/

     executable statement1;
     executable /* Comment inside a command */ statement2;
     {
          declaration4;
          #compiler directive3

          executable statement3;
          /* A declaration could not go here */
     }
}
```

What happens when this hypothetical program is compiled? Here is a short synopsis:

- The compiler performs the commands in the two compiler directives at the top of Figure 4-3.
- The compiler reserves space for the two variable declarations. It then reaches the statement main( ). When the compiler sees main( ), it knows that it has found where the program begins executing.
- The code inside of the block that follows main( ) is then translated to machine language.

Note that when the compiler reaches the third compiler directive it will perform an action that may affect the way the rest of the program is translated.

A Real Example

Now a real example. Enter the program in Figure 4-4 into the *Turbo C* editor.

Because it begins with a pound sign, you can tell that the first line in this program is a compiler directive. The include command tells the compiler to find the file stdio.h and include it in the program it is compiling.

Figure 4-4. A Real C Program

```
#include <stdio.h>          /* Include standard input/output */

main()
{
    printf("Hello, World\n");
    printf("This is my first program\n");
}
```

The file stdio.h is a special kind of file called a header file. It contains commands for input and output (its name stands for STanDard Input/Output.Header). Header files will be described in more detail later on.

Next comes the special declaration main( ). This signals that the next block is where program execution begins. Inside this block are two executable statements, both of which use the same command. This command, called printf( ), will print any text placed between the parentheses to the screen. Such text must begin and end with a pair of quotation marks.

The first statement

printf("Hello, World \ n");

will print the words *Hello, World* to the screen.

The characters \ *n* are treated specially by the printf( ) command. These two characters are equivalent to pressing the Enter key. When printf( ) sees them, it moves to the beginning of the next line.

To run this program, use F10 to go to the main menu and select the Run option. The compiler will quickly compile your program producing the screen output shown in Figure 4-5.

Figure 4-5. Screen Output

```
Hello, World
This is my first program
```

```
Press any key to return to Turbo C . . .
```

Errors

It's time to look a little more closely at the way *Turbo* C handles errors. Change the original example program so that it looks like the program in Figure 4-6.

Figure 4-6. C Program with Errors Introduced

```
include <stdio.h>          /* Include standard input/output */

main)
{
     printf("Hello, World\n);
     printf("This is my first program\n")
}
```

Four characters have been removed:

• The pound sign before include.
• The first parenthesis after main.
• The quotation mark following Hello, World \ n.
• The semicolon following the second printf( ).

Try running this program.

This is a good place to use one of the *Turbo* C shortcuts mentioned earlier. *Turbo* C allows you to select any of the main menu options, regardless of where you are, by holding down the Alt key and typing the first letter of the option you wish to select.

For example, if you're in the editor and you want to go to the File menu, simply hold down the Alt key and press the F key. (A shorthand way of writing this key combination is Alt-F. Later in the book, you'll see this combination frequently. You should understand that it means to hold down the first key and press the second key.)

You would now like to select the Run option from the editor. Instead of using F10, the cursor keys, and Enter to run the program, type Alt-R. This will invoke the compiler.

The compiler will soon find the errors. Press the space bar to leave the compilation window. The error messages will appear as in Figure 4-7.

Figure 4-7. Error Listing

```
   File      Edit     Run     Compile    Project    Options     Debug
                              ─── Edit ───
   Line 5      Col 17   Insert Indent Tab C:PROG4_1.C
Include <stdio.h>            /* Include standard input/output */

main)
{
      printf("Hello, World\n);
      printf("This is my first program\n")
}




═══════════════════════════ Message ═══════════════════════════
Compiling C:\TURBOC\PROG4_1.C:
Error C:\TURBOC\PROG4_1.C 1: Declaration syntax error
Error C:\TURBOC\PROG4_1.C 5: Unterminated string or character constant


```

F1-Help F5-Zoom F6-Edit F7/F8-Prev/Next error F9-Make F10-Main Menu

Each error message consists of three parts. The first part shows the file in which the error occurred. Following the filename is the line number where the compiler found the error. Look at the Edit window. You'll notice that one of the lines is highlighted. This is the line where the first error was found. Following the line number is the type of error that occurred. The first error was a declaration syntax error. What does that mean?

Look in the Edit window. The line

include <stdio.h>

was marked. If you remember, the original version was a compiler directive. Because you removed the # character, *Turbo C* did not recognize it as such and assumed that the command was a declaration. Since the word *include* is not a legal declaration, an error occurred. To fix this, press the F6 key. That will put you in the editor. Replace the pound sign.

One error has been fixed. What next?

Recall that F8 will show you the next error in the program. Press F8. The cursor will move to the line containing the first printf( ) statement, and the error message *Unterminated string or character constant* will be highlighted.

A string is a list of characters contained in a pair of quotation marks. Printf( ) must be given a string to print. When you removed the quotation mark from the end of the string Hello, World \n, *Turbo C* was no longer able to determine where the end of the string was. This is what it means when it refers to an Unterminated string. Replace the quotation mark at the end of the string and press F8. Since there are no more error messages, recompile the program.

After recompiling, a puzzling error message appears:

Function call missing)

It doesn't seem to make sense. The statement looks correct.

After a compiler sees a few errors, it can become confused. An error on one line may make the compiler think that there are errors in succeeding lines even if they are correct. If this occurs, the best thing to do is to try recompiling. A single error in a crucial place can often produce a great number of spurious error messages later in the program. Fixing the first error will eliminate the spurious error messages. Type Alt-R to recompile the program. Figure 4-8 shows the results.

Figure 4-8. Another Error Message

```
    File     Edit     Run     Compile     Project     Options     Debug
 ──────────────────────────────── Edit ─────────────────────────────
    Line 3      Col 6     Insert Indent Tab C:PROG4_1.C
 #include <stdio.h>           /* Include standard input/output */

 main)
 {
         printf("Hello, World\n");
         printf("This is my first program\n")
 }




 ══════════════════════════════ Message ════════════════════════════
  Compiling C:\TURBOC\PROG4_1.C:
  Error C:\TURBOC\PROG4_1.C 3: Declaration syntax error


 ────────────────────────────────────────────────────────────────────
 F1-Help  F5-Zoom  F6-Edit  F7/F8-Prev/Next error  F9-Make  F10-Main Menu
```

There is now only one error message. It highlights the word *main)* and says *Declaration syntax error*. If you'll recall, main( ) is a type of declaration. A syntax error is like a misspelling. It represents a simple error, usually a typo or missing character. In this case, it is simply a missing parenthesis. Add the parenthesis and press F8.

If you fix that error and again try to compile, you'll be prompted to fix the second error. It will be highlighted and the computer will prompt you:

```
Statement missing ;
```

Sure enough, the statement the cursor is sitting on is missing a semicolon. Add one at the end of that line.

You have fixed all the errors in the message window, so you should try to recompile. Type Alt-R.

The program should now work (Figure 4-9).

Figure 4-9. Program Works Again

```
Hello, World
This is my first program
```

```
Press any key to return to Turbo C . . .
```

As you can see, *Turbo C* allows you to find and correct errors easily.

If you use a C compiler other than *Turbo C*, be forewarned that not all compilers use the same error messages. Some compilers would have called all of the above errors Syntax Errors. Others may have completely different messages. While the designers of *Turbo C* tried to make each error message as explanatory as possible, it may take some time before you understand every error message presented to you.

Also keep in mind that compilers aren't perfect. As you saw earlier, compilers can generate messages that have little to do with the errors that caused them. In most cases, however, the compiler will tell you exactly what is wrong with the program. With a little experience, you'll be able to fix most compiler errors with ease.

Summary

In this chapter, you learned about statements. Each statement is a single action, and each statement should be placed on its own line. You learned that sets of statements that have a single purpose are called blocks. You should now understand the use and structure of compiler directives and comments, and you wrote, compiled, and ran your first C program. And finally, you were introduced to the *Turbo C* editor's helpful error-checking functions.

Section Two
C Fundamentals

Chapter 5
Variables

You have written a very simple C program. Before you can go on to write more complex programs, you must learn some of the declarative commands hinted at in the previous chapter.

Variables

Every programming language shares the concept of the variable. A variable is simply a place in which to store information. Once a variable is declared, executable statements may perform actions upon the information stored in it.

A variable in C is like a box. It is used to store objects. Differently shaped objects must be stored in differently shaped boxes, and each box can only hold a single object.

These rules are true of both boxes and variables. By thinking of variables as actual, physical locations and of data as physical objects, it is easier to understand some of the rules concerning variables.

Variables come in different types. The type of a variable determines what kind of object it can hold. The simplest of all types is the int variable (int stands for integer). An int variable can hold any whole number from −32768 to 32767, but cannot hold any fractions (these are the wrong shape to fit in the box). All of the following are legal ints:

123 523 45 −132 −74 0

None of the following would be legal ints as they all have fractional components:

4.5 ⅝ 2¼ 3.33333

Declaring variables. To create a variable, you must declare it with a declarative statement. When you declare a variable, you're telling the computer what its type is and thus what types of objects it can hold. To declare a variable, simply use the type name followed by the name of the variable. Variable names follow a simple set of rules. They must begin with a letter, and they must contain only letters, numbers, and underscores. All of the following are legal variable names:

```
i j test Count Loop1 Accounts_Receivable
```

None of the following are legal variable names, because they either begin with a number or contain illegal characters:

Illegal Variable	Reason
123	Begins with a number
1test	Begins with a number
this.is.bad huh?	Contains periods, a space, and a question mark

Though variable names may be any length, *Turbo C* will only look at the first 32 characters. As far is *Turbo C* is concerned, the following two variables are the same:

```
This_is_a_really_long_variable_used_as_an_example
This_is_a_really_long_variable_used_in_the_same_example
```

The first 32 characters in both variables are the same, so they are treated as the same variable by the compiler.

Assigning values to variables. In order to put information in a variable, you must use an assignment operator. In C, the assignment operator is the equal sign. To place the number 10 in a variable called *a* that has been previously declared as an int, you simply state that *a* equals 10:

```
a = 10;
```

Figure 5-1 is a short program that declares a single variable and then stores the number 10 in it.

Figure 5-1. Assigning a Value to a Variable

```
main()
{
    int a;

    a = 10;
}
```

The first line in this program creates an int variable called *a*. The second line of this program takes the number 10 and places it in variable *a*.

You can run this program, but it will have little effect. The program stores the number 10 in the variable *a*, but does nothing else. Nothing is ever printed to the screen to show you that the action was successful.

Printing the value of a variable to the screen can be a complicated proposition; the method for doing this will be presented later. In order to make these first few programs more interesting, here is a simple printf statement that will print the value of a single variable to the screen:

printf("The value of 'a' is %d \ n",a);

Don't worry about how this statement works. The mechanism will be described later. This statement will print the contents of the variable *a* to the screen. Figure 5-2 contains a new version of the previous example.

Try running this program. Barring typos, this should produce the output shown in Figure 5-3.

Figure 5-2. Assigning a Value to an Int Variable

```
#include <stdio.h>
main()
{
        int a;

        a = 10;
        printf("The value of 'a' is %d\n",a);
}
```

Figure 5-3. The Result of Program

```
The value of 'a' is 10
```

Press any key to return to Turbo C. . .

Variable Types

C has three types of variables. They are called

- int
- char
- float

Char. You're already familiar with the type int. The type char, which stands for character, is meant primarily for storing letters. The following are all legal characters which could be stored in a type char variable:

'a' 'r' 'y' 'q' '+' '@' '\'

Note the single quotation marks surrounding each character. These quotation marks tell C that the letter is a character and not a variable name. The method for storing characters is identical to the method for storing integers (see Figure 5-4).

Figure 5-4. Assigning a Letter to a Char-Type Variable

```
#include <stdio.h>

main()
{
    char a;

    a = 's';
    printf("The value of a is %c\n",a);
}
```

Notice that the printf( ) statement has changed slightly. Where the previous example used %d, this example uses %c. The reason for this change will be explained in Chapter 7.

The program again creates a variable called *a*, but this time it is of type char. The assignment statement then stores the letter *s* in this variable. Because the variable *a* is now of type char, this is legal. Try running this program (Figure 5-5).

Figure 5-5. Result of Running Program

```
The value of 'a' is s
```

```
Press any key to return to Turbo C. . .
```

Variables of type char can also hold certain numbers. In C, a variable can store anything of the right size. A char variable is smaller than an int variable, so while it can store numbers like an int variable, those numbers must be smaller. In fact, only integers in the range 0–255 can be stored in a variable of type char. The program in Figure 5-6 would be legal in C. (Note that printf( ) has changed back again.) Because the number 8 is small enough to fit in a char variable, the program will run normally (see Figure 5-7).

Figure 5-6. Assigning a Value in the Range 0–255 to a Char Variable

```c
#include <stdio.h>

main()
{
    char a;

    a = 8;
    printf("The value of 'a' is %d\n",a);
}
```

Figure 5-7. Result of Running Program

```
The value of 'a' is 8
```

```
Press any key to return to Turbo C. . .
```

What happens when you try to fit a larger number into a char variable? Try running the program in Figure 5-8 to find out.

Figure 5-8. Assigning a Value Greater Than 255 to a Char Value

```
#include <stdio.h>

main()
{
   char a;

   a=1024;
   printf("The value of 'a' is %d",a);
}
```

The number assigned to *a* was changed to 1024. This is too large to fit into a char variable. The result of running this program can be seen in Figure 5-9.

Figure 5-9. Result of Running Program

```
The value of 'a' is 0
```

```
Press any key to return to Turbo C. . .
```

This should have printed 1024, but instead it printed 0. This is an example of the flexibility of C creating a subtle error. In most languages, assigning a number value to a character variable would itself have resulted in an error. C allows you to make the assignment, assuming that you know what you are doing. Consequently, a false value was obtained, illustrating the importance of care in mixing variable types.

Change the char to int in the program and rerun it. It will now return the correct value (Figure 5-10).

Figure 5-10. Result When Variable Type is Changed to Int

```
The value of 'a' is 1024
```

```
Press any key to return to Turbo C. . .
```

Float. In addition to variables of type char and int, there is a third type: float. A variable of type float contains a floating-point number. A floating-point number is a number which may contain a fractional component such as

3.14 5.023 6.023E23

None of the above numbers can fully be stored in an int variable (assigning 3.14 to an int variable will store the number 3 in it). The following numbers, though integers, could also be legally assigned to floating-point variables.

3 100 99999

C will convert 3 to 3.0, 100 to 100.0, and so on. Any legal integer can be assigned to a float variable. Figure 5-11 gives an example of how a float variable can be used. (Note that printf( ) has changed again. The %d is now %f.) Try running this program (See Figure 5-12.)

Figure 5-11. Assigning a Value to a Variable of the Float Type

```
#include <stdio.h>

main()
{
    float a;

    a = 9.5345
    printf("The value of 'a' is %f",a);
}
```

Figure 5-12. Result of Running Program

```
The value of 'a' is 9.534499
```

```
Press any key to return to Turbo C. . .
```

Mixing Types

It is possible to freely mix variables of type float and int. If you assign a value of type int to a float variable, C will automatically convert the value to a float. If you assign a value of type float to an int variable, C will automatically convert the value to an int, discarding any fractional portion of the value. Figure 5-13 gives an example of this.

Figure 5-13. Program Mixing Variables

```
#include <stdio.h>

main()
{
    float a;
    int b;

    b = 10;
    a = b;
    printf("The value of 'a' is %f\n",a);
}
```

Two variables are created. The first, *a*, is of type float. The second, *b*, is of type int. The first executable line in this program puts the number 10 in the integer variable *b*. The second line assigns the contents of the integer variable *b* to the float variable *a*. C automatically converts this value from an integer to a float. The printf then prints the contents of *a*, producing the results shown in Figure 5-14.

Figure 5-14. Result of Running the Program

```
The value of 'a' is 10.000000
```

```
Press any key to return to Turbo C. . .
```

As with integer variables, there are limits to the ranges of numbers that floating-point variables can hold. This range is very large, however. Floats can range from 3.4E − 38 to 3.4E + 38 and can be either positive or negative.

Additional Variable Types

There are several variations of the basic variable types in C. There are three integer types (you saw above how a char variable is really a smaller version of the int variable) and two types of floating-point variables. Each of these takes up a different amount of space in memory (see Figure 5-15).

Figure 5-15. Sets of Variable Types

Integer Types	Floating-Point Types	Size
Char		1 byte
Int		2 bytes
Long	Float	4 bytes
	Double	8 bytes

Bytes. All variables come in sizes that are multiples of one byte. A byte is the computer's basic unit of storage. Every computer has memory made up of a certain number of bytes. A *kilobyte* consists of exactly 1024 bytes. If your machine is a 256K machine, then it has 256 × 1024 (or approximately 256,000) bytes of memory. As you can see, a standard 640K IBM XT has a fairly large memory.

Ranges. Variables that use a larger number of bytes can contain larger numbers. The various ranges of int variable types are listed in Figure 5-16.

Figure 5-16. Ranges of Variables of the Int Type

Type	Low	High
Char	0	255
Int	−32,768	32,767
Long	−2,147,843,648	2,147,843,647

Ints, chars, and longs. Ints can be used for most applications. Char variables are usually used only for characters. Longs (short for *long integers*) are usually used only when very large numbers must be dealt with.

Floats and doubles. Floats also come in different sizes. For a floating-point variable, this is reflected not so much in the size that the variable can take, but in how accurately the number is stored (see Figure 5-17). Remember that any operation, such as addition and multiplication, performed on integers and within the range of int-type variables will be absolutely accurate. This is not so with floating-point variables. Why? A floating-point number has only a given number of digits of accuracy. In real-life situations, there is no such limit on accuracy. Take the number ⅓ for example. We know that this is represented in decimal by 0.3 followed by an infinite number of 3's, but the computer can store only a limited amount of information. If you assign a number like this to a variable, the computer will do its best: It will round off the number and assign it to the variable. The variable will contain a number close to the number you intended, but it will not be *exactly* what you wanted.

Figure 5-17. Ranges and Accuracy of Float Variable Types

Type	Low	High	Approximate Accuracy
Float	3.4E−38	3.4E+38	7 digits
Double	1.7E−308	1.7E+308	14 digits

Why are floats not accurate? In theory, there are an infinite number of floating-point numbers:

4.5 4.55 4.555 4.55555555 4.5555555555555555

There is no way any computer could store all possible floating-point numbers in memory. Once again, most computers will round a floating-point number to a number that it can store. This is represented by the number of digits of accuracy. In the example above, the second two numbers would be converted to 4.555556 if they were stored in a float-type variable. A double (short for *double-precision variable*) would do somewhat better. All but the last number would be stored accurately; the last would be converted to 4.55555555555556.

Using longs in place of doubles. If accuracy is important, doubles should be used. If doubles are not accurate enough, then you should try to think of a way to use ints or longs instead, as these are always completely accurate within their range.

A good example of how this can be done is seen in a program that deals with money. You might be tempted to store money in a float variable; after all, money has a fractional component. This can be very risky. When dealing with large amounts of money, you'd start to lose pennies. Or your program may start telling you things like:

You have $4362.3333333.

This can be avoided if you simply think of money as a number of pennies rather than a number of dollars. You can never have a fractional number of pennies. Therefore, integer variables or longs can be used. This way, your results will be totally accurate. Integer variables are always accurate so you'll never lose pennies.

There is another reason that integers and longs are preferable to floats and doubles. The computer performs operations on floating-point variables much more slowly than on integer variables. Floating-point variables should only be used when you definitely need a fractional component.

Near and Far Pointers. There is another type of variable, mentioned here just to make the list of variable types complete. This type is called a pointer, and it also comes in two types: near and far. This completes the set of all basic types as shown in Figure 5-18. Pointers will be described in more detail in subsequent chapters.

Figure 5-18. A Complete List of Variable Types

Size	Integer	Real	Pointer
1 byte	Char		
2 bytes	Int		Near pointer
4 bytes	Long	Float	Far pointer
8 bytes		Double	

Macros

A C macro provides a convenient method for substituting a name for a given value. Macro definitions provide a simple method for naming commonly used values.

A macro definition is not a C statement. Instead, it is a compiler directive much like the #include statement in the program you wrote earlier. The syntax of such a definition is as follows:

`#define name value`

This tells the compiler to replace all occurrences of *name* with the specified value. Both *name* and *value* may be any string of characters. Figure 5-19 gives an example of how a macro might be defined.

Figure 5-19. Using a Macro to Assign a Value

```
#include <stdio.h>
#define PI 3.1415                          /* Set value for PI */

main()
{
    float b = PI;
    float a;

    a = PI;

    printf("The value of 'a' is %f\n",a);
    printf("The value of 'a' is %f\n",PI);
}
```

In Figure 5-19, a #define statement assigns the number 3.1415 to the name PI. When this program is compiled, all occurrences of PI will be replaced with 3.1415. This changes two of the statements:

a = PI;

becomes

a = 3.1415;

and

printf("The value of 'a' is %f\n",PI);

becomes

printf("The value of 'a' is %f\n",3.1415);

Summary

In this chapter, you saw how macro definitions can be used to assign names to numbers, improving the readability of your programs. You also learned the basic types of variables and some variations of them. Variables allow you to store information in the memory of the machine. The next few chapters will show you how you can manipulate the information in these variables.

Chapter 6
Mathematical Expressions

In most computer languages, one of the easiest tasks to perform is the manipulation of mathematical expressions. C is no exception. The C language can be used for virtually every mathematical application. The tools available in C allow the programmer to use almost any type of math, from arithmetic to calculus.

Addition, Subtraction, Multiplication, and Division

This chapter will show you the foundation of mathematics in C. As you'll see in subsequent chapters, these mathematical tools are used in virtually every program.

Most mathematical expressions are written in C just as you'd write them on paper. Such expressions are then converted by C into a value. For example, the following expression could be used to add two numbers:

```
2 + 3
```

C will treat the above expression just as it would any other number. It is not a complete statement, however. You need to do something with the value that you're calculating. A mathematical expression is a value, so you can assign it to a variable just like any other number:

```
a = 2 + 3;
```

This will add 2 and 3 and put the results in the variable a. Figure 6-1 illustrates this. Try running this program. The variable a will take on the value of 5 (Figure 6-2).

Figure 6-1. Assigning a Value to a Variable via an Expression

```c
#include <stdio.h>

main()
{
    int a;

    a = 2 + 3;
    printf("The value of 'a' is %d\n",a);
}
```

Figure 6-2. Results of Running Program

```
The value of 'a' is 5
```

```
Press any key to return to Turbo C. . .
```

You may use any of the four basic mathematical operations. As you might suspect, the symbols $+$ and $-$ stand for
addition and subtraction, respectively. An asterisk (*) stands
for multiplication, and the slash (/) stands for division.

Try running the program after substituting different operators in the previous example (Figure 6-3).

Figure 6-3. Results of Running Program with Different Operators

```
a = 2 + 3        produces        "The value of 'a' is 5"
a = 2 - 3        produces        "The value of 'a' is -1"
a = 2 * 3        produces        "The value of 'a' is 6"
a = 2 / 3        produces        "The value of 'a' is 0"
```

What happened to the division example? You know that 2 divided by 3 certainly isn't 0.

Remember that *a* is an int variable. The number 2 divided by 3 produces a value of 0.6666666. This is not an integer, so C must convert it into a whole number before it will fit into the variable *a*. In the process, the fractional component is lost, thus 0.6666666 becomes 0.

Try changing the variable *a* to a float. (Remember to change the printf( ) also.) Figure 6-4 illustrates what the program will look like after the change. Run the program to see the results (Figure 6-5). This is a little closer to what you expected.

Figure 6-4. Converting *a* to a Float

```
#include <stdio.h>
main()
{
     float a;

     a = 2.0 / 3.0;
     printf("The value of 'a' is %f\n",a);
}
```

Figure 6-5. Floating-Point Results

```
The value of 'a' is 0.666667
```

```
Press any key to return to Turbo C. . .
```

Modulus

There is a fifth operator in C that gives the remainder of a division operation. This is the modulus operator. C uses the percent character to stand for modulus. The modulus of two numbers is the remainder produced when one number is divided by another. For example, consider the expression

5 % 2

The number 5 is evenly divisible by 2 exactly two times, leaving a remainder of 1, therefore the modulus of 5 and 2 is 1. Figures 6-6 through 6-8 contain some examples of the modulus operator. In Figure 6-6, the value of *a* will be 1.

Figure 6-6. Modulus Example 1

```
#include <stdio.h>

main()
{
        int a;

        a = 5 % 2;
        printf("The value of 'a' is %d\n",a);
}
```

Figure 6-7. Modulus Example 2

```
#include <stdio.h>

main()
{
        int a;

        a = 6 % 3;
        printf("The value of 'a' is %d\n",a);
}
```

Figure 6-8. Modulus Example 3

```
#include <stdio.h>

main()
{
        int a;
        a = 2 % 6;
        printf("The value of 'a' is %d\n",a);
}
```

Because 3 goes into 6 evenly, there is no remainder. Thus *a* has a value of 0 in Figure 6-7. Because 6 does not go into 2 at all, there is a remainder of 2. The value of *a* will be 2 in Figure 6-8.

Precedence

C can easily handle much more complicated expressions. For example, consider the program in Figure 6-9.

Figure 6-9. A More Complex Expression in C

```
#include <stdio.h>

main()
{
        float a;

        a = 5 + 6 * 7 / 2;
        printf("The value of 'a' is %f\n",a);
}
```

What value will this produce? Operators in C (just like operators in math) have a quality called *precedence*. Operators with higher precedence are evaluated first. Figure 6-10 contains a list of the five main operators in order of precedence:

Figure 6-10. Precedence in C Math

Operator	Precedence
* / %	First
+ −	Last

Division, multiplication, and modulus all have equal precedence. This precedence is greater than the precedence of addition and subtraction. If a choice must be made between two operators of the same precedence (such as in the case of 5 + 6 − 4), the expression is evaluated from left to right.

a = 5 + 6 * 7 / 2;

In this expression, both multiplication and division have a precedence greater than that of addition so one of these two operations must be performed first. The multiplication is leftmost, so it is evaluated first, producing 42.

a = 5 + 42 / 2;

Of the remaining two operations, division has the highest precedence so the expression 42 / 2 is evaluated next, producing a value of 21.

a = 5 + 21;

Finally, this is added to 5, producing 26.

a = 26;

This value is then assigned to the variable *a*. Figure 6-11 contains the output from the program in Figure 6-9.

Figure 6-11. Results of Expression in Figure 6-9

```
The value of 'a' is 26.000000
```

```
Press any key to return to Turbo C. . .
```

These rules of precedence are identical to the rules of precedence used in mathematics and, just as in mathematics, you may use parentheses to force the expression to be evaluated in any order you choose. Anything within parentheses is evaluated first (within the parentheses, the precedence rules determine what is evaluated first). You could modify the preceding expression in such a way that the computer is forced to do the addition first, then the multiplication, and then the division (see Figure 6-12).

Figure 6-12. Imposing Order of Precedence with Parentheses

```
#include <stdio.h>

main()

{

        float a;

        a = ((5 + 6) * 7) / 2;

        printf("The value of 'a' is %f\n",a);

}
```

What will this produce? The inner set of parentheses is around the expression (5 + 6), so *Turbo C* will first add these two numbers, producing 11. It will then move to the next outer set of parentheses, evaluating ((11) * 7) to produce 77. Finally, it will divide the result of these operations by 2, producing a value of 38.

Using Variables in Expressions

Variables may also be used in expressions. C will then use the contents of that variable to evaluate the expression.

In Figure 6-14, you'll see a new way of declaring variables. Until now, all declarations you have seen took this form:

type name;

It is possible to create more than one variable of a certain type simply by listing them after the type, separated by commas:

type name1,name2,name3;

Figure 6-13. Declaring Multiple Variables and Using Them in Expressions

```
#include <stdio.h>

main()
{
        int x,y,a;

        x = 4;
        y = 2;
        a = x * x + y * y;
        printf("The value of 'a' is %d\n",a);
}
```

In the current example, you declare three variables, all of type int, called *x*, *y*, and *a*.

int x,y,a;

Note that all names must be different. The following statement would cause an error message:

int a,b,a;

This is because the variable *a* is declared twice. This restriction still stands even if the declarations are on different lines:

int a;
int b;
int a;

There is an exception to this restriction which will be discussed later in this book.

Back to the example. When *Turbo C* sees the expression

a = x * x + y * y

it realizes that *x* and *y* are not numbers, and it immediately looks for variables named *x* and *y*. When it finds these variables, it replaces each of them with its current value. With *x* set to equal 4 and *y* to equal 2, the expression above evaluates to

a = 4 * 4 + 2 * 2

This is evaluated like any other numeric expression, producing the value 20. This is then stored in the variable *a*.

This will only work for declared variables. Try removing the declarations from this program as in Figure 6-14.

Figure 6-14. Trying to Run a Program Without Declaring Variables

```
#include <stdio.h>

main()
{
        int a;

        x = 4;
        y = 2;
        a = x * x + y * y;
        printf("The value of 'a' is %d\n",a);
}
```

This program does not tell the computer what the letters *x* and *y* refer to. When you try to compile this program, *Turbo C* becomes confused and tells you that these are undefined symbols. C does not know what type of variables they are, so it cannot use them.

You should also make sure that you never take things out of a variable before you put anything into it. Consider Figure 6-15.

Figure 6-15. Trying to Run a Program Without Assigning Values to Variables

```
#include <stdio.h>

main()
{
        int a,x,y;

        y = 2;
        a = x * x + y * y;
        printf("The value of 'a' is %d\n",a);
}
```

This example is the same as figure 6-13 except that nothing was stored in *x*. What will *Turbo C* do with this? Try running it.

The program will compile and run. This is strange. You might not expect the program to work. What output does it produce? See Figure 6-16. Press the space bar and look in the Message window (shown in Figure 6-17).

Figure 6-16. Results of Running Program

```
The value of 'a' is 680
```

```
Press any key to return to Turbo C. . .
```

Figure 6-17. Message Window After Running Program

```
      File      Edit      Run      Compile    Project      Options      Debug
                                   ─ Edit ─
      Line 8      Col 44    Insert Indent Tab  C:PROG6_8.C

  main()
  (
                  int x,y,a;

                  y = 2;
                  a = x * x + y * y;
                  printf("The value of 'a' is %d\n",a);
  )



  ═════════════════════════ Message ═════════════════════════
  Compiling C:\TURBOC\PROG6_8.C:
  Warning C:\TURBOC\PROG6_8.C 8: Possible use of 'x' before definition in funct
  Warning C:\TURBOC\PROG6_8.C 8: Possible use of 'x' before definition in funct
  Linking PROG6_8.EXE:

  F1-Help  F5-Zoom  F6-Edit  F7/F8-Prev/Next error  F9-Make  F10-Main Men SCROLL
```

The messages that appear here are not error messages. Rather, they are warnings. A warning message shows you anything that *Turbo C* thinks might be a problem but does not consider an error. *Turbo C* thinks that x may not contain a value when the line

```
a = x * x + y * y
```

is executed, but it is not quite sure. It informs you that this might be a problem but compiles the program anyway.

You might think *Turbo C* would assume that x contained a value of 0. After all, 0 is almost the same as nothing. Evaluate the formula

```
a = x * x + y * y
```

It becomes

```
0 * 0 + 2 * 2 = 4
```

Did the machine produce a value of 4? Probably not. Before you place anything into a variable, its contents are un- defined. In *Turbo C*, a variable might contain 0 when declared. The key word is *might*. Every once in a while another number will appear in x. For example, when the author ran the above example, the program gave the following message:

```
The value of 'a' is 293
```

When you ran the program, you probably received a com- pletely different number. That's why it's important that you always assign values to variables before you attempt to take anything out of the variable. Otherwise, you'll receive a ran- dom result. *Turbo C* will warn you when you take a value from a variable that has had nothing assigned to it. You should pay attention to these warnings. They are intended to help you.

In order to prevent such problems, *Turbo C* allows you to initialize variables when they are declared. This stores a value in a variable before any statements are executed. This is done in a statement that looks somewhat like a combination of an assignment and a standard variable declaration:

```
type name1 = value;
```

or

```
type name1 = value1, name2 = value2;
```

Try adding this feature to the previous example (see figure 6-18).

Figure 6-18. Declaring and Assigning Variables at the Same Time

```
#include <stdio.h>

main()
{
        int a,x=0,y=0;

        y = 2;
        a = x * x + y * y;
        printf("The value of 'a' is %d\n",a);
}
```

In this example, as soon as the variables x and y are created, the number 0 is stored in them. Now, regardless of what happens in the rest of the program, you can be guaranteed of the contents of these variables. Try running this program. This time, the results cannot vary (Figure 6-19).

Figure 6-19. Results of Running Program

```
The value of 'a' is 4
```

```
Press any key to return to Turbo C. . .
```

Both x and y start out as 0. The variable a is undefined (you don't know what is in it). The first executable statement changes the value of y to 2. The second executable statement evaluates the expression

a = x * x + y * y

and replaces variables with values to get

a = 0 * 0 + 2 * 2

This produces the value 4 which is stored in the variable a.

Summary

As you can see, there are some subtle traps to watch for when using variables. *Turbo C* will help you avoid them by giving you warnings, but because C is such an open language, it cannot protect you completely. You should also be aware that C is not perfect. It will sometimes issue a warning when none is needed or remain silent when a warning might be helpful. This should only happen in more obscure applications so you should not be too concerned with it at this point.

Chapter 7
Calling Functions

A solid understanding of standard C functions is an important part of C programming. While the C command set is large, there are a number of things that cannot be done using these commands. Printing to the screen, using the disk drives, and performing complex math cannot be done easily without standard functions. Obviously these functions are important. A standard function is technically not part of C itself. It is a routine that is used with C.

You've already seen one example of a standard function. As stated earlier, C uses standard functions to print to the screen. Printf( ) is one such function. You have used printf( ) in previous examples, but its syntax was not described.

Earlier in this text, you were told that the include file stdio.h allowed you to print to the screen. The purpose of this file will now become more clear.

Libraries

In order to use a standard function, you must first tell C where its definition can be found. This is done in the #include compiler directive. The file stdio.h actually contains a set of declarative statements that tell C where to find routines that do certain things such as printing to the screen.

These sets of commands are held together in header files. These files are marked with a trailing .h. Each header file will contain declarations for a group of similar standard functions. So far you have only used the header file stdio.h. This file allows C to use any of the standard input/output functions. Any time the program must read from the keyboard, write to the screen, or write to or read from the disk, you'll need to use one of the functions declared in this file. Because nearly every program will need to print to the screen, nearly every program will include this file.

There are a number of different sets of standard functions (usually called libraries). Some of these, such as math.h or string.h are part of the standard C implementation and can be found on nearly any C system. Others, such as dos.h and dir.h are specific to the IBM PC and can be found in many different C compilers for the IBM PC. Others, such as float.h, are specific to *Turbo C*.

Many of these libraries are concerned with advanced programming techniques that are beyond the scope of this book. Others are commonly used in even the simplest programs. In this chapter, you'll be shown routines found in four important libraries:

stdio.h   The single most important library in C. It handles all high-level input and output for a program.

math.h   For any mathematical application. This library lets you use many important mathematical functions, such as tangent, sine, and cosine.

ctype.h   A set of short routines that check the type of a variable. You could, for instance check to see whether a character variable contains a punctuation mark.

stdlib.h   A set of miscellaneous routines that produce random numbers, sort lists, exit to DOS, or perform other useful actions.

C Functions

A properly designed program breaks a large problem down into smaller tasks. C supports this idea with *functions*. A function is a section of code designed to do a specific task. A function may or may not receive parameters (values). If parameters are present, it will perform some operation on them. When the function is finished, it may or may not return a value. Once written and debugged, a function can be used in other programs without having to start over from scratch.

You've already seen one such function (Figure 7-1). Printf( ) is a C function that takes at least one parameter—a string of characters. It then prints these characters to the screen and returns to the main program without passing back a value.

Figure 7-1. Printf( ) Takes a Value, Performs an Action, and Returns No Value

```
{
    printf("Hello, World!");
    printf("This is my first program");
}
```

This conforms to the basic syntax of all C functions. The function name is followed by a list of parameters inside a set of parentheses. Note that even if there are no parameters, you still need the parentheses.

Figure 7-2 contains an example of a function that returns a value. It takes one parameter (a character) and returns a value (its lowercase equivalent).

Figure 7-2. Tolower( ) Function Returns a Value to the Program

```
#include <stdio.h>
#include <ctype.h>

main()
{
    char a,b;

    b = 'F';
    a = tolower(b);
    printf("The value of 'a' is %c",a);
}
```

The function tolower( ) is in the C library ctype.h. If you use this function in a program you must include the line

```
#include <ctype.h>
```

Tolower( ) sends a value to the main program. In order for the program to use this value, it must assign the value to a variable.

Compile and run this program. The variable *a* will contain the character *f*. Your program sent the value contained in the variable *b* (the uppercase letter *F*) to the function tolower( ). Tolower then returned the lowercase equivalent of that letter (the lowercase character *f*) to the main program. The main program then stored this value in the variable *a* with an assignment statement.

In the previous example, you sent the letter to be converted to the function tolower( ) in the variable *b*. This was not necessary. Parameters can be passed either as variables or values. You could send the letter *F* directly to tolower( ) as in Figure 7-3.

Figure 7-3. Sending *F* Directly

```
#include <stdio.h>
#include <ctype.h>

main()
{
    char a,b;

    a = tolower('F');
    printf("The value of 'a' is %c",a);
}
```

Printf( )

In the first few chapters of this book, you wrote short programs to print the values of variables to the screen. You've been shown examples of printf( ) that will work for specific cases, but the full use of the printf( ) function was never fully explained. The printf( ) function is actually a general-purpose format conversion function. Here is a printf( ) statement you're already familiar with:

printf("The value of 'a' is %d\n",a);

This function call has two parameters. The first is a character string: *The value of 'a' is %d\n*. The % sign indicates where the second parameter will be substituted and what form it will be printed in.

Format specification. You have probably noticed that when the string is printed to the screen, the characters %d were replaced with the value contained in *a*. These two characters constitute a format specification. They show the printf( ) function where the contents of variable *a* should be printed. When this statement is executed, the value in the variable *a* replaces the characters %d in the format string, so if *a* is set equal to 5, the following transformation occurs:

The value of 'a' is %d\n

becomes

The value of 'a' is 5\n

There are a number of different format specifications. In each case, the percent sign signals that a value is to be printed at a certain position. The letter that follows the percent sign shows the type of value to be displayed. Consider the three types of variables that you have used, shown in Figure 7-4.

Figure 7-4. Variable Type and Format Specification

```
char                    %c
int                     %d
float                   %f
```

If you look back at the examples in the previous chapters, you'll notice that whenever *a* contained an integer, the string *The value of 'a' is %d\n* was used. If *a* was a character, the string was *The value of 'a' is %c\n.*

In many cases, the type of variable printed need not match the format specification used. Only the class of variable is important, not the size. This means that a variable of type char can be printed as either an integer or a character. Try the example in Figure 7-5.

Figure 7-5. Printing a Character Either as a Char or an Int

```
#include <stdio.h>

main()
{
    char a = 'A';

    printf("'a' is %c or %d\n",a,a);
}
```

In this example, the value of *a* is printed twice, once as a character and once as an integer. The variable *a* is assigned the character *A* so you know what the first format specification will print. What will happen when you try to print the letter *A* as an integer? You'll discover that both *A* and the number 65 (the ASCII value for *A*) will be printed.

ASCII value. On the IBM PC, every character is assigned a certain number. This is called its ASCII value. Every letter is stored in the machine's memory as an ASCII value. The character *A*, for example, is stored as the number 65. Many languages will try to hide this fact from you by refusing to let you treat characters as numbers. C, on the other hand, allows you direct access to this function. You can print a character as a number or a number as a character with no difficulty (see Figure 7-6).

Figure 7-6. Printing a Small Integer as a Char or an Int

```
#include <stdio.h>

main()
{
     int a = 65;

     printf("'a' is %c or %d\n",a,a);
}
```

Run this program. Notice that the results do not change. In C, the integer 65 is treated identically to the letter *A*. When the program is translated into machine language, the following two lines are identical:

a = 'A'

and

a = 65

Number of formats. It's important that there always be at least one variable per format specification. An extra format specification will produce strange results. For example, the printf( ) in Figure 7-7 has one too many format specifications.

Figure 7-7. A Function Call with Too Many Format Specifications

```
#include <stdio.h>

main()
{
     int a = 5;

  printf("'a' is %d or %d",a);
}
```

This might produce something reasonable, like

'a' is 5 or 0

It is more likely, however, that this will produce something like

'a' is 5 or −4216

As you may have guessed, the reason for this is similar to the problem you saw before with uninitialized variables. Since there are two %d's in the format string, printf( ) is expecting two variables. You have only given it one. It will get the second one from some random place in memory whose value cannot be guaranteed.

You're allowed to have more variables than format specifications. These extra variables are simply ignored.

There is one last unexplained area in your earlier programs. Consider the string:

"The value of 'a' is %d\n"

The sequence \n is the *newline* character. When printed, it performs a carriage return (advances output to the next line), just as if you had pressed the Enter key.

Figure 7-8 shows a pair of printf( ) statements that don't use \n. Try running the program.

Figure 7-8. Printf( ) without Carriage Return

```
#include <stdio.h>

main()
{
      printf("Here is the first thing");
      printf("Here is the second thing");
}
```

This will print out as

```
Here is the first thingHere is the second thing
```

All of the text stays on one line. The \n tells the IBM PC to go to the beginning of the next line. The backslash (backwards slash) character signals that the following character is a special character. Modify your program as shown in Figure 7-9.

Figure 7-9. Program Modified to Provide Carriage Return

```
#include <stdio.h>

main()
{
        printf("Here is the first thing\n");
        printf("Here is the second thing");
}
```

This will now produce much more understandable results:

```
Here is the first thing
Here is the second thing
```

It may seem a little awkward to have to remember to use this character to go to the next line, but you'll find that you use it so often that it quickly becomes natural to stick the extra \n on the end of every string. By not automatically moving to the next line, C gives you more power over screen output. You could use many printf( )s to print a single line as in Figure 7-10. You could also print many lines with one printf( ) as in Figure 7-11.

Figure 7-10. Forming a Single Line of Text with Multiple Printf( ) Statements

```
printf("This ");
printf("is ");
printf("one ");
printf("Line\n");
```

```
Would print:

        This is one line
```

Figure 7-11. Printing Multiple Lines of Text with One Printf( ) Statement

```
printf("Line 1\nLine 2\nLine 3\nLine4\n");
```

would print:

```
        Line 1
        Line 2
        Line 3
        Line 4
```

Scanf( )

One other commonly used I/O (Input/Output) function is scanf( ). It's very similar to printf( ). While printf( ) is used to print text and values to the screen, scanf( ) is used to read values from the keyboard. The parameters used with scanf( ) follow the same rules as those used with printf( ), with one important exception.

Both functions use format strings. The format specification for scanf( ) is usually simpler, however, because it doesn't make much sense to try to read a particular set of characters, as in

scanf("Hi there!");

This is perfectly legal C and will compile. It will not produce reasonable results when run, however. This statement tells the computer to read the characters *Hi there!* from the keyboard. Obviously, if you knew what the user was going to type, you wouldn't need to read from the keyboard in the first place.

The format strings for scanf( ) usually consist only of format specifications, as in

scanf("%d",&answer);

This statement will read an integer and place it into the variable called *answer*. Now you can see the major difference between printf( ) and scanf( ). Printf( ) requires a format string and a list of variables. Scanf( ) requires a format string and a list of variable names prefixed with ampersands (&). The reasons behind this will become clearer in later chapters, but for now, simply remember that every variable in a scanf( ) statement must be prefixed with an ampersand. Figure 7-12 contains an example of scanf( ).

Figure 7-12. Use of Scanf( ) in Program

```
#include <stdio.h>

main()
{
    int number;

    scanf("%d",&number);
    printf("The number is %d\n",number);
}
```

Now run this program. When the program runs, all activity will stop, and the cursor will move to the upper left corner of the screen. The scanf( ) statement waits for you to type a number. Type a number and press Enter. The printf( ) function will then print *The number is* and the number you just typed.

There is no limit to the number of things that may be read using one scanf( ) statement (see Figure 7-13).

Figure 7-13. Receiving More than One Piece of Information with a Single Scanf( )
Statement

```
#include

main()
{
        char ch1,ch2,ch3,ch4;

        scanf("%c%c%c%c",&ch1,&ch2,&ch3,&ch4);
        printf("%c%c%c%c",ch4,ch3,ch2,ch1);
}
```

Now run this program. Press any four letters and press
Enter. These letters will be printed in the reverse order in
which you just typed them. (Notice that the variables are
listed in different orders in the printf( ) and scanf( ) functions.)

The way scanf( ) reads values into variables can be a little
difficult to understand at first. To get a better understanding,
you should look at what the computer actually does when values are typed from the keyboard.

The scanf( ) function won't read anything until the Enter
key is pressed. As soon as the Enter key is pressed, scanf( )
starts reading the keys that were typed. Look at Figure 7-14.

Figure 7-14. Example Program with Scanf( ) Function

```
#include <stdio.h>

main()
{
    int a,b,c,d;

    scanf("%d%d",&a,&b);
    scanf("%d%d",&c,&d);
    printf("%d %d %d %d",d,c,b,a);
}
```

Enter four numbers separated by spaces and press Enter.
When you type the four numbers, nothing happens. Then,
when Enter is pressed, the four numbers are sent to the program. The first scanf( ) statement is looking for two numbers,
so it reads the first two numbers you typed, storing them in
the variables *a* and *b*. The second scanf( ) sees that there are
two numbers left. It is waiting for two numbers, so it takes

these and places them in the variables *c* and *d*. Only after the two scanf( ) statements have been executed can the printf( ) statement print these numbers in reverse order.

Now run the program again, this time only typing a single number and pressing Enter. Nothing happens. Why?

When you press the Enter key this time, only one number was waiting to be read. The first scanf( ) was expecting two, so it read the first, storing it in *a*. Then it waits for a second number.

Now type two more numbers and press Enter. Still nothing will happen. The first scanf( ) sees the new numbers. It only needs to read one more, so it reads one of the two numbers and places it in *b*. The next scanf( ) then gets a chance to execute. This scanf( ) reads the remaining number and places it in *c*. It still needs another number, so it will stop everything to wait for the final number.

Now try typing two more numbers. The first four numbers will be printed in reverse order.

The second scanf( ) was waiting for a single number so the first of the two numbers was read and placed in the variable *d*. After that, the printf( ) was reached, and it printed the first four numbers in reverse order. Because there isn't another scanf( ) in the program, the last number you typed is ignored completely.

Different types of values have different rules concerning how they must be separated when read by scanf( ). The numeric formats are the easiest. Each number must be separated by spaces, tabs, or carriage returns. For example, the four numbers in the previous example could have been entered like this:

12 13 14 15

or like this:

12
13
14
15

or like this:

12   13
14
15

Or in any other similar combination. Floating-point numbers are separated in the same way:

12.41   414.51
525.73
486.1538

Try modifying your program to use floating-point numbers, as in Figure 7-15.

Figure 7-15. Using Scanf( ) with Floats

```
#include <stdio.h>

main()
{
    float a,b,c,d;

    scanf("%f%f",&a,&b);
    scanf("%f%f",&c,&d);
    printf("%f %f %f %f",d,c,b,a);
}
```

Now run the program. It works like the previous example, except that it uses floating-point numbers.

What would happen if you used floating-point numbers in the original integer example? Try the program in figure 7-16 with the following input:

1.1 2.2 3.3 4.4

When this is run, it produces the output shown in Figure 7-16.

Figure 7-16. Meaningless Output When Floats Are Input to Int Variables

```
1.1 2.2 3.3 4.4
40 23294 24 1
```

Press any key to return to Turbo C. . .

The output isn't exactly what was expected. While C is very good at changing floats to integers and vice versa, the printf( ) function is not. If printf( ) is expecting an integer and you send it a floating-point number, it becomes confused. Even more importantly, the format specification must be of the same class as the variable. Try running the program in Figure 7-17. Not only will this not read characters correctly, it will produce the error message shown in Figure 7-18.

Figure 7-17. Mixing Format Specifications and Variable Types

```
#include <stdio.h>

main()
{
     int a,b,c,d;

     scanf("%f%f",&a,&b);
     scanf("%f%f",&c,&d);
     printf("%f %f %f %f",d,c,b,a);
}
```

Figure 7-18. Error Message Generated by Program

```
scanf : floating point formats not linked
Abnormal program termination
```

```
Press any key to return to Turbo C. . .
```

This is a new kind of error called a runtime error. Unlike a compiler error, which occurs when the program is first translated, a runtime error occurs after compilation when the program is used.

This highlights the difference between C statements and C functions. In general, C statements will always convert variables and values to the appropriate type before using them. Functions, like printf( ), may or may not convert a variable or value to the right type, depending upon the function. When you read the chapter on building your own functions, you'll begin to see why.

Characters

Character variables work slightly differently from numeric variables. If you look back at the first example of scanf( ), you'll realize that character values need not be separated by a space. Run that original example (in Figure 7-13) and use the following input:

a b c d

Make sure the letters are separated by spaces. This is four characters, right? What will the output be? You might expect that the program would print the first four characters in reverse order. But the program prints

b a

What happened? Only two characters were printed. The reason for this, as you may already have guessed, is that a character in C is anything that can be produced from the keyboard. A space is a legal character. What the scanf( ) function saw was

a(space)b(space)c(space)d(enter)

It assigned the first four characters to variables as follows:

Variable	Value
a	a
b	space
c	b
d	space

These were sent to printf( ) which printed

(space)b(space)a

Even the Enter key is treated as a separate character. Once again, run the program in Figure 7-13 and type the following:

a
b
c
d

Before you can press the *c* key, the program will print

b
a

The reason for this result is the same as with the previous example. First you typed *a* and Enter. When the Enter key was pressed, scanf( ) saw two characters, the *a*, which it stored in the variable *a*, and the Enter, which it stored in the variable *b*. You then typed the letter *b* and Enter. The second scanf( ) then stored the letter *b* in the variable *c* and stored Enter in *d*. At that point, the printf( ) was reached so it printed the characters in reverse order. You were not given a chance to enter the rest of the characters.

Obviously characters cannot be entered if scanf( ) is expecting integers. This will produce the same odd results that you get when fractional numbers are entered as integers. Here is an example. Consider these three values:

586.0878
123
Fred

Now consider what the three format specifications would do with each of these.

First, the %d specification is the pickiest. When it sees the first value 586.0878, it becomes confused because the value is not an integer. It can handle the next value with no trouble. It's an integer and that's what it expects to see. When it sees *Fred* it becomes confused again, because *Fred* is not an integer.

Now consider %f. This specification is looking for a floating-point number. The first value is a floating point number, so it has no difficulty. The next can also be thought of as a floating-point number, so %f can read it. The last value is not a number at all, so %f becomes just as confused as %d did.

Now consider %c. This specification will read anything at all, but only one character at a time. When %c sees 586.0878, it sees it as eight characters, 5, 8, 6, ., 0, 7, and 8. In a similar manner, 123 is seen as 1, 2, and 3, and *Fred* is seen as *F, r, e,* and *d.* Any possible input can be handled since anything typed from the keyboard is a legal character. Figure 7-19 shows a summary of this principle.

Figure 7-19. Table of Input Accepted by Various Input Specifications

	Whole Number	Decimal Number	Letters
'%d'	Yes	No	No
'%f'	Yes	Yes	No
'%c'	Yes*	Yes*	Yes*

*will read only one character or digit.

Summary

This chapter has given you a brief overview of how standard functions may be called. It also contains a more extensive description of two important input/output functions. In the following chapters, you'll be shown many examples of these functions in use in actual programs.

Chapter 8
More About the Editor

You've already been given some basic instructions on how to use the editor. You know how to move around the file using the cursor keys, and you can insert text by typing. These commands are easy to use and remember. In addition, you may have already discovered that PgUp, PgDn, Home, and End can also be used to move the cursor around the file more quickly.

The *Turbo C* editor is very powerful. It's far more powerful than you might imagine, given the simple commands you've seen so far. The *Turbo C* editor has most of the features found in popular word processors. In fact, the *Turbo C* editor uses the same commands as *Wordstar*. If you already know *Wordstar* commands, you may want to skim this chapter as it will be mostly review.

Run *Turbo C* and load one of the example programs created in the previous chapter.

Enter the File menu and look at the options. Some of the options have function keys associated with them. For example, to the right of the load option is F3. This indicates that F3 may be used from anywhere in *Turbo C* to load a file. Leave the File menu and enter the editor by typing Alt-E. Now press the F3 key. The load-file option will be invoked just as if you had picked the load option from the menu (Figure 8-1).

Figure 8-1. Pressing F3 Will Invoke File Loader

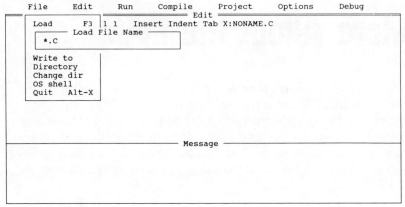

The Keypad

The cursor-movement keys can be found on the keypad at the right end of the computer keyboard. When Num Lock is off, these keys allow you to move the cursor. When Num Lock is on, these keys print numbers. If you see numbers when you press one of these keys, press the Num Lock key so that the following examples will work as expected.

Most of these keys will do exactly what you'd expect them to do. The cursor keys will move you one space left, right, up, or down. These keys correspond to the *Wordstar* commands Ctrl-S, Ctrl-D, Ctrl-E, and Ctrl-X (Figure 8-2).

Figure 8-2. Cursor-Key Command Equivalents

```
Ctrl-S          Left Arrow
Ctrl-D          Right Arrow
Ctrl-E          Up Arrow
Ctrl-X          Down Arrow
```

If you're accustomed to *Wordstar,* the control commands may be used instead of the cursor keys. Both key sequences will have the same effect in *Turbo C.* Experiment with this. While you're in the *Turbo C* editor, use the down cursor key to move down a line. Now try moving up a line with Ctrl-E. Now move up another line using the up key. Move to the right with Ctrl-D for awhile.

Paging

The PgUp and PgDn keys will also do what you'd expect: PgUp will move the cursor up one complete page (one screen) in the file, and PgDn will move the cursor down one page (one screen) in the file. You may use the *Wordstar* commands Ctrl-R and Ctrl-C as substitutes for PgUp and PgDn, respectively, if these are easier for you to remember.

The Home and End keys are equivalent to the Ctrl-Q,S and Ctrl-Q,D *Wordstar* key sequences (in which you'd press the Ctrl and Q keys simultaneously and then press either S or D). The Home key will move the cursor to the beginning of the line. The End key will move the cursor to the end of the line. Again, this is what you'd expect given the names of these keys.

Changing Text

There are two other very important keys on the keypad. The Del key will remove the letter under the cursor. Note that this isn't the same as what the Backspace key does. The backspace key removes the character immediately to the left of the cursor.

For example, consider the first sentence in Figure 8-3.

Figure 8-3. Sample Text

```
Cursors, Foiled again!



Cursos, Foiled again!



Curss, Foiled again!
```

The cursor is sitting on the second letter *r* in the word *Cursors*. If you press the Del key, you'll remove that letter. (See Figure 8-3, line 2.)

The cursor is now sitting on the letter *s*. If you were to press the Del key again, the *s* would be removed. Instead press the Backspace key. The *o* will be removed (Figure 8-3, line 3).

Insert and Overwrite Mode

The *Turbo* C editor works in two different modes: insert and overwrite. The effect of entering text from the keyboard depends on which mode the editor is in. The Ins key toggles between insert and overwrite modes. This is equivalent to the *Wordstar* Ctrl-V key combination.

Up to now, you've been working in insert mode exclusively, since that is the editor's default condition. Any character you type moves all the characters after the new character one space to the right.

In overwrite mode, new characters are typed on top of old characters. Old characters are not moved aside to make room for new characters.

Figure 8-4 is a simple example to illustrate the modes.

Figure 8-4. Sample Text

```
      File     Edit     Run    Compile    Project    Options    Debug
                              ═══════ Edit ═══════
    ┌───────────────────────────────────────────────────────────────┐
    │    Line 1     Col 1   Insert Indent Tab C:FIG8_3.C             │
    │The first rule of programming:                                   │
    │                                                                 │
    │        "You can't always do what you want                       │
    │         but you usually get what you need"                      │
    │                                                                 │
    │The second rule of programming:                                  │
    │                                                                 │
    │        "It's always a good idea to have                         │
    │         lots of cool games"                                     │
    │                                                                 │
    │                                                                 │
    │                          ──── Message ────                      │
    ├─────────────────────────────────────────────────────────────── ┤
    │                                                                 │
    │                                                                 │
    │                                                                 │
    └───────────────────────────────────────────────────────────────┘
      F1-Help  F5-Zoom  F6-Edit  F9-Make  F10-Main Menu
```

Look at the line at the top of the edit window. This is the window status line. You should see the column and line numbers and the word *Insert*. This signifies that the editor is in insert mode. Cursor down to the third line of the example and position the cursor between the words *you* and *need*. Now type the word *really*. Notice that the word *need* is moved to the right to make way for the new word (Figure 8-5).

Figure 8-5. The Word *really* Inserted into Text

```
    File      Edit      Run      Compile    Project    Options    Debug
                                === Edit ===
      Line 4      Col 46   Insert Indent Tab C:FIG8_3.C
The first rule of programming:

        "You can't always do what you want
         but you usually get what you really need"




                              ─ Message ─



```
F1-Help F5-Zoom F6-Message F9-Make F10-Main menu

Now, using the backspace key, remove the word *really*
and press the Ins key. The word *Insert* will disappear from the
window status line. Now type the word *want* (Figure 8-6).

Figure 8-6. The Word *want* Overwrites the Word *need*

```
    File      Edit      Run      Compile    Project    Options    Debug
                                === Edit ===
      Line 4      Col 43   Insert Indent Tab C:FIG8_3.C
The first rule of programming:

        "You can't always do what you want
         but you usually get what you want"




                              ─ Message ─



```
F1-Help F5-Zoom F6-Message F9-Make F10-Main menu

The word *want* replaces the word *need*. The advantage of
this mode is that you need not delete a word to replace it.

Advanced Features

These simple commands are enough to accomplish most programming tasks. There are, however, a great number of other commands that give you greater flexibility. Don't worry if you can't remember all of these commands at first. Very few people have the memory or the patience to digest the entire command set all at once. The basic commands located on the keypad are sufficient to allow you to edit a file. As you gain experience, you'll pick up some of the more complex commands.

Moving by Words

The Ctrl-A and Ctrl-F commands allow you to move more rapidly within a line of text. These commands are the word-move commands. Ctrl-A will move the cursor one word to the left, and Ctrl-F will move the cursor one word to the right. A word consists of any number of characters not separated by spaces or punctuation. Figure 8-7 contains some possible words.

Figure 8-7. Collections of Characters Considered Single Words

```
word
number1
a_long_function_name
asgasga
```

Suppose the cursor were on the first letter of the word *were* in the following phrase:

```
and then there were none
```

Typing Ctrl-A would move the cursor to the first letter in the word *there*. On the other hand, typing Ctrl-F would move the cursor to the first letter in the word *none*.

Moving the Screen

The Ctrl-W and Ctrl-Z commands allow you to move the text on the screen without changing the cursor location. These commands are the scroll commands. Ctrl-W will move the entire screen down one line, exposing a new line at the top of the window. The Ctrl-Z command will move the entire screen up one line, exposing a new line at the bottom of the window. In either case, the cursor remains at its current location. These commands allow you to view other parts of the file without moving the cursor.

Deleting Text

While Backspace and Del are usually sufficient to remove unwanted text, the editor provides a few more powerful commands. The delete-word command allows you to delete a
word of text. (Remember that a word consists of any number
of characters not separated by spaces or punctuation.) Consider the following line:

Isn't this loads of fun?

If you moved the cursor to the letter *l* in *loads* and typed
Ctrl-T, the delete-word command, the line then would look
like this:

Isn't this of fun?

The cursor would now be located on the letter *o*. Try Ctrl-
T again. This should remove the next full word, which is *of*:

Isn't this fun?

This command only deletes letters to the right of the
cursor even if it is in the middle of a word. Move the cursor to
the letter *n* in *Isn't* and type Ctrl-T. The line will become

Is this fun?

It's also possible to delete an entire line of text or to delete everything from the cursor to the end of a line. Ctrl-Y will
remove whatever line the cursor is currently on.

Figure 8-8. Sample Text

```
      File      Edit      Run      Compile    Project     Options     Debug
                                   ═══ Edit ═══
      Line 4      Col 43   Insert  Indent Tab C:FIG8_3.C
   The first rule of programming:

           "You can't always do what you want
            but you usually get what you want"

   The second rule of programming:

           "It's always a good idea to have
            all appropriate business software, avoid having
            lots of cool games"



   ─────────────────────────── Message ───────────────────────────




   F1-Help  F5-Zoom  F6-Message  F9-Make  F10-Main menu
```

97

In Figure 8-8, if you move to the line beginning with *All appropriate* and press Ctrl-Y, you'll remove the line, and the text shown in Figure 8-9 results.

Figure 8-9. Text Altered by Ctrl-Y

```
    File      Edit      Run      Compile      Project      Options      Debug
                                  ═ Edit ═
    Line 9        Col 10   Insert Indent Tab C:FIG8_3.C
The first rule of programming:

        "You can't always do what you want
         but you usually get what you want"

The second rule of programming:

        "It's always a good idea to have
         lots of cool games"




─────────────────────────────── Message ───────────────────────────────




F1-Help  F5-Zoom  F6-Message  F9-Make  F10-Main menu
```

Also, pressing the sequence Ctrl-Q,Y will delete everything from the cursor to the end of the line. Suppose the cursor were on the first letter *o* in the line

screen=0;oops this is a mistake.

Press Ctrl-Q. A special key-combination symbol (^Q) will appear at the top of the screen. This symbol indicates that the editor is awaiting an additional keypress. Now press the Y key. This will change the previous line to read

screen=0;

The *Turbo C* editor improves on *Wordstar* by taking many of the confusing key sequences (for instance, Ctrl-Q,S) used to perform simple functions and assigning them to numeric keypad keys (for instance, the Home key).

Summary

You'll find the great majority of commands you use are located on the keypad. This command subset gives you enough power to write and edit most small- to medium-sized programs. Later in this book, additional commands will be described that make managing even the largest files a simple task.

Section Three
Control Structures

Chapter 9
Control Statements

Control statements control the flow of a program. So far, all the programs you've seen were completely linear. The flow ran in one direction only, from the first statement to the last. Execution begins at the top, and each statement is performed exactly once, one at a time (see Figure 9-1).

Figure 9-1. The Flow Through a Linear Program

If this were the only way to write programs, computers wouldn't be very useful. There are two things that make a computer an important piece of hardware. The first is decision-making. To say that computers can make decisions means that they are able to make choices (and thereby change program flow) based on conditions. The second important property of computers is their ability to perform the same task thousands or even millions of times. This second property is called looping.

101

Three Categories of Control Structures

There are three main categories of control structures.

- *If statements* allow different sets of statements to be executed under different conditions.
- *Loops* allow a set of statements to be repeated a number of times.
- *Functions* allow a set of statements to be used from a number of different places in a program.

Each control structure contains one statement or a block of statements which it controls. As you saw before, any set of legal C statements surrounded by brackets is a block. For example:

```
{
    a=a+1;
    c=a+b;
}
```

While it is not a requirement of the C language, most programmers will indent all statements contained in a block to offset them from the surrounding program text. Additionally, most programmers use only single statements on a given line even though this is not a requirement of the language. Compare the following two blocks:

Block 1
```
{
    a=a+1;
    c=a+b;
}
```

Block 2
```
{a=a+1; c=a+b;}
```

Both are perfectly legal though, in the midst of a hundred similar lines, the second might be more difficult to read.

If Statements

The *if* statement is one of the simplest of the different types of control statements in C. An *if* statement checks an expression, and if that expression is true, the statement it controls is executed. If the expression is false, the statement is ignored completely. The *if* statement has two forms. The first form of an *if* statement is

if(expression)
    statement;

The expression can include numbers, variables, or mathematical expressions. The following expression will be true when the number contained in *a* is equal to 0:

a == 0

Otherwise, it will be false.

The following expression will be true only if the number contained in *a* is the same as the number contained in *b*. It will be false otherwise.

a == b

Here is an example of a simple *if* statement:

if(a==0)
    printf("A is zero \ n");

When the statement is executed, the value of the variable *a* is compared with the number 0. If equals 0 (that is, if *a* contains the number 0) this expression will be true, and the printf( ) statement will be executed. Figure 9-2 contains an example of this.

Figure 9-2. Program with an *If* Statement

```
main()
{
    int a;

    printf("Enter the value of 'a' here :");
    scanf("%d",&a);
    if(a==0)
        printf("A is zero\n");
}
```

Run this program and enter the number 0. The program should print the words *A is zero* on the screen. Because *a* was set to 0, the expression

a == 0

is true, and the words are printed.

Try running the program again, this time entering the number 1 when prompted. Because the expression is no longer true (*a* no longer contains 0), the printf( ) statement is not executed, and nothing is printed to the screen.

Notice that there is no semicolon after the conditional statement. The statement that immediately follows an *if* statement is considered part of the *if* statement. You might be interested to know that a semicolon by itself is a legal C statement. Such a statement does nothing, but it is legal. If you had placed a semicolon at the end of the *if* statement, nothing would be executed when the expression was true. The following line would be seen by the compiler to mean *if* a *contains a zero, then do nothing:*

if(a==0);

The program would then continue executing the next statement.

Add a semicolon to the *if* statement in Figure 9-2. Now run the program, entering different values for the variable *a*. Notice that the printf( ) is executed regardless of the value you enter. Because of the semicolon at the end of the *if* statement, the printf( ) statement is no longer considered part of the *if* statement. This extra semicolon is a common error in C, especially among novice programmers.

Multiple statements. Multiple statements may be controlled by an *if* statement. Just replace the single statement with a block containing many statements (Figure 9-3). Run this program and enter a 0. Figure 9-4 shows the results.

Figure 9-3. Multiple Statements with an *If* Statement

```
#include <stdio.h>

main()
{
    int a;

    printf("Enter the value of 'a'");
    scanf("%d",&a);
    if(a == 0)
    {
        printf("A is a zero\n");
        printf("Printing the value of a\n");
        printf("%d",a);
    }
}
```

Figure 9-4. Results of Running Program

```
Enter the value of 'a'0
A is a zero
Printing the value of a
0
```

Run the program again, this time entering a value other
than 0. Nothing at all will be printed to the screen.

When C was designed, it was decided that double equal
signs (= =) would be used for comparison and a single equal
sign (=) would be used for assignments. This can cause subtle
errors. For example, the following statement looks superficially
correct:

if(a=0)

It is in fact a legal C statement, though it will not do what
you might expect. Just as the statement

a = = 0

returns a value, so does

a = 0

It will assign a value of 0 to *a* and return this value as the
value of the expression. In C, false is represented by the number 0. Thus the statement a = 0 would always be considered
false. If you use an assignment instead of an expression in an
if statement, *Turbo* C will issue the warning shown in Figure
9-5.

Figure 9-5. Error Message Returned When Assignment Is Found Where Expression
Is Expected

```
    File     Edit     Run     Compile     Project     Options     Debug
                                  Edit
      Line 9      Col 15   Insert Indent Tab C:PROG9_2.C
main()
{
      int a;

      printf("Enter the value of 'a'");
      scanf("%d",&a);
      if(a = 0)
      {
            printf("A is a zero\n");
            printf("Printing the value of a\n");
            printf("%d",a);
      }
}
                             Message
 Compiling C:\TURBOC\PROG9_2.C:
 Warning C:\TURBOC\PROG9_2.C 9: Possibly incorrect assignment in function main
 Linking PROG9_2.EXE:


 F1-Help  F5-Zoom  F6-Edit  F7/F8-Prev/Next error  F9-Make  F10-Main Menu
```

The message is that there is a *possibly incorrect assignment,* which implies that the assignment might be correct. Why would anyone want to do an assignment in an *if* statement? Wouldn't this always be a mistake? Not necessarily.

Often functions will return true if they succeed and false if they fail. For example, the function atoi( ) converts a string to a number. If this function is not able to convert the string to a number, it returns false. The following statement would convert the string "451" to the number 451 and return true:

atoi("451");

All of the following statements return false as they are not numbers:

atoi(" ");
atoi("Fred");
atoi("Not a number");

Suppose you wanted to convert a string to a number and place it in the variable *num*. Now suppose that you wanted this variable to be printed to the screen only if the string was in fact a number (see Figure 9-6).

Figure 9-6. An Example Program Using an Assignment in an Expression

```
#include <stdio.h>

main()
{
     int num;

     if(num=atoi("592"))        /* Not '==' !!! */
          printf("The string is the number %d\n",num);
}
```

The expression converts the string "592" to an integer and stores the value in the variable *num*. If it succeeds, it returns true, otherwise it returns false. If the statement num = atoi("592") is true, then the value in *num* is printed on the screen. Otherwise nothing is printed. Note that this will not work if the value 0 is placed between the quotation marks. The way this statement is written, Turbo C is unable to tell the difference between a value of 0 and a false statement.

Modify the *if* statement so that the string is no longer a number:

if(num=atoi("Fred"))

Run this program. The number is no longer printed. This example was somewhat contrived, and it's unlikely that you'll make assignments within expressions until you're more experienced. But you must be aware of the possibility of misusing a single equal sign within an expression. And also be aware that there is a reason C allows this construct.

Relational Operators

There are a number of other tests available to you besides the equality operator (==):

Example **Meaning**

$a < b$ Less than. This statement is true if the value contained in a is less than the value contained in b.

$a > b$ Greater than. This statement is true if the value contained in a is greater than the value contained in b.

$a <= b$ Less than or equal. This statement is true if the value contained in a is less than or equal to the value contained in b.

$a >= b$ Greater than or equal. This statement is true if the value contained in a is greater than or equal to the value contained in b.

$a != b$ Not equal. This statement is true if the value contained in a does not equal the value contained in b.

For all these operators, either a or b may be replaced with any variable, value, or expression (Figure 9-7).

Figure 9-7. Statements Using Conditional Operators

```
a >= 53
42 <= 1
a + 42 != c + d
3 + 5 == 90 - fred
```

Consider the following example:

a != b + c

This would return true only if the sum of the numbers contained in *b* and *c* does not equal the number contained in *a*. Figure 9-8 provides an example of this.

Figure 9-8. Program Example Using Inequality in *If* Statement

```
#include <stdio.h>

main()
{
    int a,b;
    a = 4;
    b = 5;
    if(a+b == 5)
        printf("Doesn't add up to five");
}
```

If-Else

Often *if* statements are used to cause program flow to branch in one of two different directions. This cannot be done with the first form of the *if* statement. With the first *if* statement, flow will always look like Figure 9-9.

Figure 9-9. Program Flow with *If* Statement

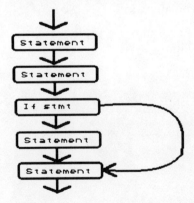

As mentioned above, the *if* statement has another form—the *if-else* statement. This form allows you to branch in the manner shown in Figure 9-10.

Figure 9-10. Program Flow with *If-Else* Statement

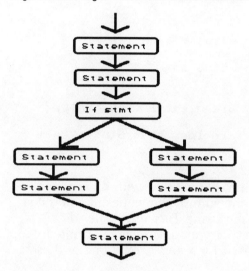

Here is the syntax for an *if-else* statement:

```
if(expression)
    statement1;
else
    statement2;
```

This statement will do one of two things:

• If the expression is true, statement1 will be executed.
• If the expression is false, statement2 will be executed.

In any case, only one of the two statements will be executed. As with the first form of the *if* statement, multiple statements may be controlled by an *if-else* statement. Just replace the single statement with a block containing many statements.

Figure 9-11 contains an example of how an *if-else* statement might be used.

Figure 9-11. Program Example Using an *If-Else* Statement

```
#include <stdio.h>

main()
{
     int a,b;

     printf("Enter the value for 'a':\n");
     scanf("%d",&a);
     printf("Enter the value for 'b':\n");
     scanf("%d",&b);
     if(a+b >= 5)
          printf("They are greater than 4\n");
     else
          printf("They are less than 5\n");
}
```

Try running this program. Experiment with different values for *a* and *b*. Whenever the sum of the values in *a* and *b* is greater than or equal to 5, the string *They are greater than 4* is printed, otherwise the string *They are less than 5* is printed. No matter what values are chosen for *a* and *b*, only one of these two strings will be printed.

Complex Expressions

Often you'll need to test two or more expressions to create a complex expression. You may do this by using the logical *and* (&&) and the logical *or* (||) operators. These operators are used to tie two or more expressions together to create a single, large expression. For example, the logical *and* operator returns a value of true if and only if both of the expressions it connects are true:

To test whether two variables are equal to 0:

if(a==0 && b==0)

In this case, if both *a* and *b* equal 0, this condition will return true. If either of these expressions is false (that is, if either *a* or *b* is not equal to 0), then this expression will be false.

Figure 9-12. Sample Program Demonstrating Logical *And* Operator

```
#include <stdio.h>

main()
{
     int a,b;

     printf("Enter the value for 'a':\n");
     scanf("%d",&a);
     printf("Enter the value for 'b':\n");
     scanf("%d",&b);
     if(a == 5 && b == 234)
         printf("Both values meet the conditions\n");
}
```

Try running the program in Figure 9-12 a few times. Experiment with different values for *a* and *b*. The printf( ) statement will be executed only when both *a* and *b* have the correct values.

The logical *or* operator, symbolized by double vertical bars (‖), returns true if either of the expressions it connects is true. Consider the following statement:

if(a==0 ‖ b==0)

This will return true if either *a* is equal to 0 *or* if *b* is equal to 0. This expression will return false only if *a* is not equal to 0 and *b* is not equal to 0. Run the program in Figure 9-13 a few times. The printf( ) will be executed if either *a* or *b* is 0.

Figure 9-13. Sample Program Demonstrating Logical *Or* Operator

```
#include <stdio.h>

main()
{
     int a,b;

     printf("Enter the value for 'a':\n");
     scanf("%d",&a);
     printf("Enter the value for 'b':\n");
     scanf("%d",&b);
     if(a == 0 || b == 0)
         printf("One of these is zero\n");
}
```

In this chapter, you've learned about a large number of relational operators (==, !=, <, >, <=, >=) and logical operators (||, &&). These operators are very similar to the arithmetic operators described earlier in the book. Like arithmetic operators, relational and logical operators return values. The *if* statement actually needs only a single value in the parentheses:

```
if(value)
    statement;
```

If the value is true, the statement is executed. In C, any nonzero number represents true. Zero represents false. The relational and logical operators return either true (usually −1) or false (0). Often programmers will add the following two macro definitions to the beginning of their files:

```
#define TRUE −1
#define FALSE 0
```

This allows the programmer to manipulate the words *true* and *false* rather than the numbers −1 and 0. This can enhance the readability of your program.

Consider this expression:

```
a == 0
```

This expression returns 0 if *a* contains any value other than 0. If *a* is 0, this expression returns −1.

The relational and logical operators have lower precedence than any of the arithmetic operators, which means that all math will be performed before any relational or logical expression will be evaluated. The table below shows an expanded precedence list (operators grouped together have the same precedence):

Symbol	Meaning	Precedence
*	Multiplication	1
/	Division	1
%	Modulus	1
+	Addition	2
−	Subtraction	2
<	Less than	3
>	Greater than	3
<=	Less than or equal to	3
>=	Greater than or equal to	3

Symbol	Meaning	Precedence
==	Equal	3
!=	Not equal	3
&&	Logical And	4
||	Logical Or	4
=	Assignment	5

The purpose of precedence is to insure the proper evaluation of expressions as the one in Figure 9-14.

Figure 9-14. Use of Precedence in a Program

```
#include <stdio.h>

main()
{
        int a=5,b=4,c=1;

        if(a + b <= c * 45)
                printf("It is true!\n");
}
```

C sees the individual expressions in the *if* statement and evaluates them according to precedence. The multiplication has the highest precedence so it is evaluated first. The value of *c* (which is 1) is multiplied by 45 to produce 45, reducing the expression to

a + b <= 45

The addition operator has the next highest precedence. The values of *a* (5) and *b* (4) are added together to produce 9, reducing the expression to

9 <= 45

There is now one final operator, the *less than or equal to* operator. This checks to see whether 9 is less than or equal to 45. It is, so the expression evaluates to true.

This is used by the *if* statement:

if(TRUE)
  printf("It is true!\n");

Because the expression is true, the string is printed.

Logical operators have a precedence even lower than relational operators (see preceding table).

This helps explain how logical operators *and* and *or* can tie together expressions. Consider the program in figure 9-15.

Figure 9-15. Logical *And* Used to Link Expressions

```
#include <stdio.h>

main()
{
    int a=0,b=3;

    if(a == 0 && b == 0)
        printf("Both are zero\n");
}
```

The == operator has a higher precedence than &&, so the two equality operators are evaluated first. This reduces the expression to

TRUE && FALSE

Since the logical *and* operator returns true if and only if both of its arguments are true, this expression returns false. This causes the *if* statement to skip over the printf( ) statement.

You may wonder what would happen if either of the arguments given to the logical *and* or *or* operators were neither true nor false. For example, what would C do with the following statement?

4321 && 623

Recall that any nonzero value is considered true by C. C would see this as

TRUE && TRUE

It would evaluate this expression as true.

Even the assignment operator has a precedence. This may seem a little odd to you, but consider the following statement:

a = 34 * x;

C knows that the assignment operator is to be performed after the multiplication, not before. This is because it has a lower precedence than any operator you've seen so far.

Summary

By now, you should have a good grasp of the basics of C expressions and how they can be used in the simplest of the C control structures. You've also learned the concept of precedence. If you understand how precedence works in C, you should be able to interpret any C expression. This will also allow you to use the various operators in C to their full potential.

Chapter 10
Loops

In the last chapter, you learned about the first major C control structure: the conditional statement. The conditional statement allows you to break the flow of a program into two different paths. You still have no way of repeating statements once they've been executed. All program flow is still basically linear, with an occasional fork in the road.

There is a second type of control structure called a *loop*. A loop will repeat a block of statements a number of times. How the number of iterations (the number of times the loop will repeat) is determined depends on the type of loop.

There are three types of loops in C:

• *While* loop
• *For* loop
• *Do* loop

Both the *for* loop and the *do* loop are variations of the *while* loop, so the *while* loop will be presented first.

The *While* Loop

As the name suggests, a *while* loop will repeat a block of statements while a condition is true. Once the condition ceases to be true, the statements controlled by the loop will no longer be executed, and the program will move on to statements following the loop. The syntax for a *while* loop is similar to that of a conditional statement except that *while* takes the place of *if:*

```
while(condition)
   block;
```

Like the conditional statement, the *while* statement will only execute the statements in its associated block if the condition is true. Unlike the *if* statement, the *while* statement will continue to execute these statements until this condition is no longer true. Figure 10-1 contains an example.

Figure 10-1. Program Incorporating a *While* Loop

```c
#include <stdio.h>

main()
{
      int a;

      a = 10;
      while(a > 0)
      {
            a = a - 1;
            printf("'a' is %d\n",a);
      }
      printf("Done with the loop\n");
}
```

The first two lines declare the variable *a* and set it equal to 10. This will be your control variable. A control variable is a variable used within a loop to control how many times the statements in the loop are repeated. The rest of the program in Figure 10-1 contains the *while* loop. In this example, two lines will be repeated:

```c
a = a - 1;
printf("A is %d \n",a);
```

The first line subtracts 1 from the loop control variable. The second line prints the current value of *a* to the screen. Because of the condition $a > 0$, these statements will be repeated as long as the number contained in variable *a* is greater than 0. Try running this program (Figure 10-2).

Each time the statements within the loop are executed, 1 is subtracted from *a*. Eventually the value of *a* will fall below 0. Because of the condition, the statements inside the loop will be executed only when *a* is greater than 0. Once it falls below this value, the loop will end, and the rest of the program will continue.

Figure 10-2. Results of Running Program

```
'a' is 9
'a' is 8
'a' is 7
'a' is 6
'a' is 5
'a' is 4
'a' is 3
'a' is 2
'a' is 1
'a' is 0
Done with the loop
```

```
Press any key to return to Turbo C. . .
```

The Infinite Loop

Because of the way a *while* loop is built, it's important that
you make sure the condition upon which the *while* loop is operating changes with each iteration. Often programmers forget
to modify one of the variables used by the condition inside the
loop. This produces an infinite loop. Figure 10-3 an example
of how such an infinite loop could occur.

Figure 10-3. An Infinite Loop

```c
#include <stdio.h>

main()
{
    int a;
    a = 10;

    while(a > 0)
    {
        printf("'a' is %d\n",a);
    }
    printf("Done with the loop\n");
}
```

In this loop, the variable *a* is never changed. Because the condition depends only on *a*, it will also never change. Try running this program (see Figure 10-4).

Figure 10-4. The Results of an Infinite Loop

```
'a' is 10
'a' is 10
'a' is 10
'a' is 10
'a' is 10
'a' is 10
'a' is 10
'a' is 10
'a' is 10
'a' is 10
'a' is 10
'a' is 10
'a' is 10
'a' is 10
'a' is 10
'a' is 10
'a' is 10
'a' is 10
'a' is 10
'a' is 10
'a' is 10
'a' is 10
'a' is 10
```

The program will continue to print *A is 10* until you press Ctrl-C, halting the program. In this case, the error is rather easy to catch, as the loop only has a single statement in it. In larger loops, however, discovering such an error can be more difficult.

Increments and Decrements

Loops are often used to repeat statements a fixed number of times. Whenever this is done, 1 will be either added to the control variable (to count up) or subtracted from the control variable (to count down). This can be done with the arithmetic operators (a=a+1 or a=a−1). C provides a shortcut method, however. The operators $++$ and $--$ are known as the *incre-ment* and *decrement* operators. These operators are known as *unary* operators because they operate on only a single variable. The $--$ operator will subtract 1 from a variable. The previous example could have been written as shown in Figure 10-5.

Figure 10-5. *While* Loop with Decrement Operator

```
#include <stdio.h>

main()
{
     int a;

     a = 10;
     while(a > 0)
     {
          a--;
          printf("'a' is %d\n",a);
     }
     printf("Done with the loop\n");
}
```

This example doesn't represent a major change from the earlier example. The advantage of these operators is that they may be used from within an expression. Each operator takes two forms:

$$--a$$
$$a--$$
$$++a$$
$$a++$$

If the operator precedes the variable, the *increment* or *decrement* is performed before the statement in which the operator appears. If the operator appears after the variable, then the operation is performed after the statement. Consider the statements in your loop from Figure 10-1:

a = a − 1;
printf(" 'a' is %d \n",a);

This could be changed to the following single statement:

printf(" 'a' is %d \n", −−a);

The decrement operator appears before the variable *a* because the decrement is to be performed before the printf( ). Consider the following statement:

printf(" 'a' is %d \n", a— —);

This would be exactly equivalent to these two statements:

printf(" 'a' is %d \n", a);
a = a — 1;

Using this feature, you can simplify the example in Figure 10-1 as shown in Figure 10-6.

Figure 10-6. Another *While* Loop with Decrement Operator

```
#include <stdio.h>

main()
{
     int a;

     a = 10;
     while(a > 0)
          printf("'a' is %d\n",--a);
     printf("Done with the loop\n");
}
```

These operators act slightly different from most operators because they are actually not part of the expression in which they appear. They are said to have a precedence greater than any of the other operators you've seen so far because they are always separated from the expression before any calculations are made. As an example, consider the following expression:

a = c++ * 53 + sum_of_hours;

Because ++ has the highest precedence, this expression becomes

a = c * 53 + sum_of_hours;
c = c + 1;

Note that c++ has no bearing on the value of *a*. This is the most important thing to understand about the increment and decrement operators. They are not actually part of the statement in which they appear. Consider the following statement:

a = ++c * 53 + sum_of_hours;

In this statement, the $++$ operator does have an effect on *a* as the statement will become the following pair of statements:

```
c = c + 1;
a = c * 53 + sum_of_hours;
```

Because *c* is incremented before the main expression, it will have an effect on the final value of *a*.

One final note about these operators: Because C never requires spaces with its expressions, an increment or decrement can make some of these expressions unclear. Consider Figure 10-7.

Figure 10-7. Ambiguous Use of Pre- or Post-Increment

```
#include <stdio.h>

main()
{
        int a=2,b=2,c;

        c = a+++b;
        printf("'a' is %d,'b' is %d,'c' is %d\n",a,b,c);
}
```

The expression $c = a + + + b$ is ambiguous. It could be broken down as $c = a++ + b$. In this case, *a* would be added to *b* and placed in *c*. After this, *a* would be incremented and the following statement printed:

'a' is 3,'b' is 2,'c' is 4

If, on the other hand, the expression were read as $c = a+ + +b$, *b* would be incremented, added to *a*, and placed in *c*:

'a' is 2,'b' is 3,'c' is 5

Try running the program. As you can see, C ties the increment to the variable *a*, not the variable *b*. When given a choice, C will always try to tie an increment or decrement operator to the variable on its left rather than the variable on its right. Most programmers use either spaces or parentheses to avoid confusion:

```
c = a++ +b;
```

or

```
c = (a++)+b;
```

In these cases, you can easily tell to which variable the + + operator is tied. If you follow this example, you won't have to remember precedence rules.

As a general rule, whenever you're unsure exactly how an expression should be broken down, use parentheses to organize the expression. Not only will this ensure that the expression is evaluated as you intended, it will make the expression more understandable for anyone reading your program.

The *For* Loop

A second type of loop simplifies some program control. The *for* loop is not as flexible as the *while* loop, but it's easier to understand and use. Take a look at the original *while* loop in Figure 10-1. There are two statements in this example that, while not actually part of the *while* statement, are important to its proper execution. First of all, in order for this loop to work correctly, the variable *a* must be initialized:

```
a = 10;
```

Secondly, in order to ensure that the loop terminates properly, the variable *a* must be modified somewhere inside the loop:

```
a--;
```

These statements are not part of the *while* statement, but they are still necessary to the loop as a whole. In general, all loops must have three different sections in order to operate.

• First, the initial state must be set *(a = 10;)*.
• Next, there must be some way to modify that state *(a --;)*.
• Finally, there must be a way to test this state to see whether or not the loop should stop execution *(a > 0)*.

While loops are flexible in that they don't check to see that the first two sections actually exist. You're required only to supply the condition. This gives you more flexibility on how you determine the initial state and then modify it during each iteration.

For loops require all three sections to be explicitly stated in the loop. The syntax of a *for* loop is

```
for(initial state;condition;modifying statements)
   block;
```

In Figure 10-8, the *for* loop is exactly equivalent to the *while* loop presented earlier in this chapter.

Figure 10-8. *For* Loop with *Decrement* Operator

```
#include <stdio.h>

main()
{
        int a;

        for(a = 10;a > 0;a--)
                printf("A is %d\n");
        printf("Done with the loop\n");
}
```

You no longer need the curly brackets as the block now only has a single statement in it. Run this program. It will produce the same results as the *while* loop (see Figure 10-9).

Figure 10-9. Results of Running Program

```
A is 10
A is 9
A is 8
A is 7
A is 6
A is 5
A is 4
A is 3
A is 2
A is 1
Done with the loop
```

```
Press any key to return to Turbo C. . .
```

Because all of the information involved in the loop is in the *for* statement itself, it's easier to understand than a *while* loop.

Given what has been said, you might assume that it's impossible to get an infinite loop with the *for* statement. Actually, it's quite possible to get such an error, though the error will be much more obvious. A *for* loop takes three statements—any three statements. Remember that in C, a single semicolon is a legal statement:

```
for(a = 10;a< 0;)
  printf("A is %d\n");
```

This is the same infinite loop as the infinite *while* loop presented earlier in the chapter. This is a fairly difficult mistake to make, however, as all three statements are located in one spot. You can see at a glance that this statement is incorrect.

Why does C allow such incorrect *for* statements to be compiled? There are times when such a loop might not be incorrect. You may, for example, want to have a program that never quits. Many games are written like this. Often, programmers will use an empty *for* loop to do this:

```
for(;;)
{
/* many statements */
}
```

There is no ending condition, so the loop will never end. Because there is no ending condition, there is really no need to set initial conditions or to modify any condition.

As another example, suppose you wanted to allow the user to choose the starting condition. This could be done as shown in Figure 10-10.

Figure 10-10. Allowing User to Choose Starting Condition

```
#include <stdio.h>

main()
{
        int a;

        printf("Enter the starting number:");
        scanf("%d",&a);
        for(;a > 0;a--)
                printf("A is %d\n",a);
        printf("Done with the loop\n");
}
```

Try running this program. You've left out the initial condition portion, so *a* will take on whatever value it originally had—in this case, the value the user enters.

For the most part, *while* loops and *for* loops can perform the same actions. However, certain types of loops are superior for specific tasks because of the way each is structured. The examples in this chapter have shown a loop that was best expressed as a *for* loop. Figure 10-11 shows an example of a fairly common loop that can be expressed just as well either way.

Figure 10-11. *For* Loop or *While* Loop Would Work Equally Well in This Program (*While* Loop Used)

```
#include <stdio.h>

main()
{
        char ch=0;
        while(ch != 'q')
        {
                printf("Starting loop\n");

                /*   Lots of statements */

                printf("Type 'q' to quit, any other key to continue:");
                ch=getch();
                printf("\n");
        }
}
```

This program will repeat any statements placed in the same block as the comment line until the letter *q* is typed at the *Type q to quit* prompt. The getch( ) function is used to read the key that is typed. Getch( ) is a special function that waits for a key to be pressed and then returns that key. Unlike printf( ) or scanf( ), getch( ) does not wait for the Enter key to be pressed. Figure 10-12 shows how this might be done in a *for* loop.

Figure 10-12. Same Program with *For* Loop

```
#include <stdio.h>

main()
{
        char ch;
        for(ch=0;ch != 'q';ch=getch())
        {
                printf("Starting loop\n");

                /* lots of statements */

                printf("Type 'q' to quit, any other key to continue:");
                printf("\n");
        }
}
```

In both cases, the initial condition is established by setting the variable *ch* to 0. Then, each time through the loop, the variable *ch* is modified by the statement *ch=getch( )*.

For loops are used primarily where only a single variable changes. Figure 10-13 contains a *while* loop in which two variables change.

Figure 10-13. *While* Loop with Two Variables

```
#include <stdio.h>

main()
{
     int a,b;
     a=0;
     b=100;
     while(a != b)
     {
          printf("Enter first number\n");
          scanf("%d",&a);
          printf("Enter second number\n");
          scanf("%d",&b);
     }
     printf("Those numbers are equal\n");
}
```

This program would be very difficult to write using a *for* loop; it is possible, however. Each of the three sections in a *for* loop can contain a number of statements separated by commas. Converting the previous example into a *for* loop would result in the program in Figure 10-14.

Figure 10-14. Same Program with *For* Loop

```
for(a=0,b=100; a!=b;)
{
    printf("Enter the first number\n");
    scanf("%d",&a);
    printf("Enter the second number\n");
    scanf("%d",&b);
}
```

Obviously this is stretching the *for* loop a little farther than it was intended to go. No programmer would ever opt for the second example over the first. It is more difficult to write and harder to understand. Most C programmers use *for* loops in applications where the endpoint of the loop is known when the program is written. Usually, they will be used in situations like this:

for(i=0;i<10;i++)

This loop will execute exactly ten times. You can see this just from looking at the loop statement. A single variable is moved through a number of steps one by one. *While* loops are usually used when the variables in the condition can be changed in a number of different ways:

while(i<10 && ch != 'q')

There is no easy way of telling how many times the statements in this loop will be executed without looking closely at the rest of the statements in the loop.

The *Do* Loop

The third type of loop is the *do* loop. It is a very simple modification of the *while* loop. A *while* loop (as well as a *for* loop) always checks the ending conditions before the loop is executed. The *do* loop always checks the ending conditions after the loop is executed. The primary effect of this is that statements in a *do* loop are always executed at least once, whereas statements in a *while* loop could possibly never be executed. The syntax for a *do* loop is as follows:

```
do
    block;
while(condition);
```

As with the *while* loop, statements in the block will be executed while the condition is true. Unlike the *while* statement, the statements in the block will be executed once before the condition is checked.

The *repeat until 'q'* example shown in Figure 10-12 would actually make more sense if it were written as a *do* loop. Because you only call getch( ) inside the loop, *ch* will not contain a *q* before the loop is entered. Because *ch* must contain something before the condition, it is set to 0. This loop would be better written as a *do* loop as in Figure 10-15.

Figure 10-15. Program Incorporating a *Do* Loop

```
#include <stdio.h>

main()
{
      int ch;
      do
      {
            printf("Hit 'q' to quit\n");
            ch=getch();
      }
      while(ch != 'q');
      printf("Done with the loop");
}
```

When the computer first enters the loop, *ch* is undefined. A message is printed to the screen. Next, the function getch( ) stores a value in *ch*. This initializes it. The computer has then reached the end of the loop. The contents of *ch* are compared with the letter *q*. If they are not the same, the statements inside the *do* loop will be executed again. This process continues until the value contained in *ch* is *q*.

You can use functions like getch( ) in any expression, so there is really no reason to use the variable *ch* at all (Figure 10-16).

Figure 10-16. Same Program Without Variable

```
#include <stdio.h>

main()
{
    do
    {
        printf("Hit 'q' to quit\n");

    }
    while(getch() != 'q');
    printf("Done with the loop");
}
```

For many applications, *while* loops and *do* loops can be used interchangeably. The only difference between the two types of loops is that in the *while* loop, the condition is checked at the beginning of the loop; with the *do* loop, it is checked at the end of the loop.

Summary

Each of these loops has different uses. The *while* loop is generally reserved for situations where the loop may continue for an indefinite time or where more than one variable is changed within the loop. The *for* loop is usually used when a loop should be executed a given number of times, and it is best used with a single changing variable. The *do* loop is similar to the *while* loop, except that it is used when a loop must be executed at least once (it is conceivable that a *while* loop in a program might never be executed).

In many languages, each different type of loop is distinct from the others, with its own set of applications. In C, all types of loops are very flexible and allow some overlap. This feature increases the power of each type of loop, but it also means that you could choose the wrong type of loop and thereby make programming very difficult for yourself. In most cases, the choice will be obvious.

Chapter 11
Functions

So far, all of your programs have consisted of a single unit. Program flow could branch off in different directions or loop back toward the beginning of the program as in Figure 11-1.

Figure 11-1. Program Flow with Branches and Loops

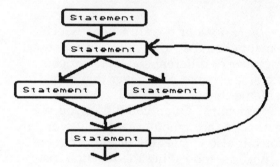

If similar tasks needed to be performed at different places in the program, the necessary commands would have to be repeated. Functions help you avoid this situation.

Functions

Functions allow you to break your code into discrete, easily understood pieces. A function gives a name to a group of statements which may then be used from a number of different places within the program as shown in Figure 11-2.

You've already used built-in C functions, such as printf( ) to perform certain tasks. You probably thought of such functions as a simple statement, like the PRINT statement in BASIC. But printf( ) is not a simple statement. The definition for printf( ) actually consists of hundreds of lines of C code. Whenever your program calls printf( ), all of these C statements are executed.

Figure 11-2. Program Flow with Branches, Loops, and Functions

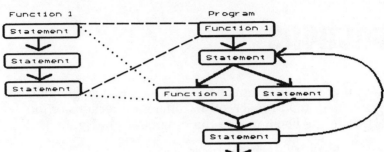

In C, it is possible to create your own functions which then can be used in a manner similar to the built-in functions. These functions tie a number of different statements together and place them under a single name. Whenever that name is used, all of those statements then are executed.

Why have separate functions? Often you'll find yourself repeating similar lines of code throughout a program. Not only does this become tedious, it also creates inefficient programs. Placing this code in a function and calling the function instead makes your program smaller and easier to debug.

Function Declarations
Every function consists of two parts:

• Declaration
• Body

You already have some experience with function declarations. You've seen main( ), a simple function declaration. The block that follows it is the body for function main( ). The general syntax for a function is

```
return_type function_name(parameter1,. . .,parameterN)
parameter declarations;
block;
```

The return_type indicates what type of value the function will return (if any). In previous examples, function main( ) has never returned a value, and it never had any parameters, so it has always been declared as

```
main( )
block;
```

Another function might look something like this:

```
int add(a,b)
int a,b;
block;
```

The int return_type in front of this function indicates that the function will be returning an int value (most likely the sum of *a* and *b*).

Here is an example of a program that uses a simple function. You do not yet know about return types or parameters, so the program in Figure 11-3 will not have either of these.

Figure 11-3. Program with Simple Function

```
#include <stdio.h>

say_hi()
{
        printf("Hi there!\n");
        printf("This was written in a function\n");
}

main()
{
    printf("Call it once:\n");

    say_hi();

    printf("Call it a couple more times\n");

    say_hi();
    say_hi();
}
```

Before function main( ), the function say_hi( ) is declared. This function controls a block that contains two printf( ) statements. Later on in the program, the function main( ) calls this function three times. A function can be called by using a single statement consisting of the function name, parentheses, and a semicolon. Try running the program (Figure 11-4).

Figure 11-4. Results of Running Program

```
Call it once:
Hi there!
This was written in a function
Call it a couple more times
Hi there!
This was written in a function
Hi there!
This was written in a function
```

```
Press any key to return to Turbo C. . .
```

The semicolon is used by the compiler to tell the difference between function declarations and function calls. Try removing the semicolon from the second function call and rerun the program. You'll get the error shown in Figure 11-5.

Figure 11-5. Error Message Resulting from Running Program Without Semicolon

```
    File      Edit      Run      Compile    Project     Options     Debug
┌──────────────────────────────────── Edit ──────────────────────────────────┐
│    Line 18    Col 15   Insert Indent Tab  C:PROG11_5.C                       │
│                                                                             │
│      say_hi();                                                              │
│                                                                             │
│      printf("Call it a couple more times\n");                              │
│                                                                             │
│      say_hi()                                                               │
│      say_hi();                                                              │
│ )                                                                           │
│                                                                             │
│                                                                             │
│                                                                             │
├═══════════════════════════════════ Message ════════════════════════════════┤
│ Compiling C:\TURBOC\PROG11_5.C:                                            │
│ Error C:\TURBOC\PROG11_5.C 18: Statement missing ; in function main        │
│                                                                             │
│                                                                             │
└─────────────────────────────────────────────────────────────────────────────┘
```

F1-Help F5-Zoom F6-Edit F7/F8-Prev/Next error F9-Make F10-Main Menu

A function declaration must never be placed inside a block. When the semicolon was removed, *Turbo C* thought that the first instance of say_hi( ) in main( ) was a function declaration and reported this as an error. This error and its converse (putting a semicolon on a function declaration) are fairly common, and the compiler will usually catch these.

The Return Statement
The return statement is used to return a value from a function. Any expression can follow return. Its syntax is

```
return(expression)
```

The calling function can ignore the returned value if it wishes.

Figure 11-6. Function with Return Statement

```
int add(a,b)
int a,b;
{
     int c;

     c = a + b;
     return c;
}
```

This program takes two values from the main program. (This is the purpose of the parameters *a* and *b*.) These are then added, and the result is placed in *c*. The function then returns this result to the main program, ending the function.

Parameters
Take a look at the function. Two of the variables, *a* and *b*, were declared outside of the braces. These variables are actually parameters. A parameter is a special variable used to pass information between a program and a function. Each of these parameters will have a value in it when the function is called by the main program. Note that the compiler did not complain that *a* and *b* were used without being initialized even though no values were ever stored in them by the function.

Before the function name is the int type declaration. This tells C that the function will return an integer to the main program. A function may return any C value type (int, char, long, double, float, and so on). A function that doesn't return a value can be declared as type *void*. This tells the compiler that the function does not return a value.

The last line in this function is the return statement. A return statement tells the computer to take the value that follows it and pass it to the main program. In this case, the function is returning the value contained in the variable *c*. The value that the function returns must be compatible with the return type used in the declaration. The function add( ) is declared to return an int, and indeed the variable *c* is an integer variable.

You already know how to call a function that has no parameters: You use the function name and a pair of parentheses. Calling a function with parameters is similar: You write the function call normally and place the parameters inside the parentheses. To retrieve values returned by a function, simply set a variable equal to the function name. Figure 11-7 contains an example of how to call the function described above.

Figure 11-7. Calling a Function and Retrieving a Value

```
main()
{
      int a;

      a = add(3,4);
      printf("Just added, 'a' is %d\n",a);
}
```

This might look a little odd to you at first, but it should soon become quite natural. The first statement calls the function add( ), sending it the numbers 3 and 4. The function add( ) receives these values as the parameters *a* and *b*. It then adds these values and places the result (7) in the variable *c*. The return statement then sends this value back to the program. Because of the assignment statement, this value is placed in the variable *a*.

Local Variables

It is important to realize that the *a* in the function add( ) is not the same as the *a* in main( ). All variables and parameters that you've used so far have been local variables and parameters. This means that they are only recognized inside the function in which they have been declared. No function will recognize variables or parameters declared in another function. That means it is possible to have a number of different variables in a program with the same name.

There are a number of dangers inherent in function calls. C never checks to see that functions are used correctly. For instance, even though add( ) returns a value, C does not require you to assign it to anything (Figure 11-8).

Figure 11-8. Value Lost Due to Failure to Make Assignment

```
main()
{
     add(3,4);
     printf("Just added");
}
```

In this example, the return value is not assigned to a variable. The program calls the function add( ) to add the numbers 3 and 4 and then promptly forgets the result.

Why would a programmer ever want to do this? It allows you to write more versatile functions. Many functions, especially those that involve input and output, return a value indicating whether or not the function succeeded. For instance, the function printf( ) returns a value. You've always treated printf( ) as if it returned nothing, but it does return a value: printf( ) returns the number of letters it successfully printed. Figure 11-9 contains an example of this.

Figure 11-9. Printing Return from Printf( )

```
#include <Stdio.h>

main()
{
     int a,b;
     a = 100;
     b = printf("Let's print the number %d\n",a);
     printf("Just printed %d letters",b);
}
```

When you run the program, the following output will be produced:

```
Let's print the number 100
Just printed 27 letters
```

Remember there is an extra character on the end of the first string—the newline character. This is the reason printf( ) returns a character count of 27 instead of the 26 you might expect.

Though it is rare that you'd ever want to use this information, C gives you the flexibility of either using this value or ignoring it. Most functions return integers. This is so common that if you don't specify a type in a declaration, C will assume that you want to return a value of the int type. Add( ) could have been declared with no return type as in Figure 11-10.

Figure 11-10. Add( ) with No Return Type Assumes Int Type

```
add(a,b)
int a,b;
{
     int c;

     c = a + b;
     return c;
}
```

It is usually a better practice to explicitly state the return type even if you want the function to return integers.

If you don't want a function to return a value, you should inform C by using the keyword *void*. The example in Figure 11-3 should have been written as in Figure 11-11.

As you can see, C is very flexible about such things. Even though your original function say_hi( ) was assumed to return an int, yet didn't, C was able to understand it. This flexibility accounts in part for the popularity of C.

Unfortunately, the flexibility of C can also lead to problems. For instance, C will not check to make sure that parameters are of the same type in the function call as they are in the function declaration. This can cause havoc if you're not careful. Consider the program in Figure 11-12.

Add( ) expects two ints, but the program sends it two floats. Run the program; the results are shown in Figure 11-13.

Figure 11-11. Declaring a Void Return

```
#include <stdio.h>

void say_hi()
{
        printf("Hi there!\n");
        printf("This was written in a function\n");
}

main()
{
    printf("Call it once:\n");

    say_hi();

    printf("Call it a couple more times\n");

    say_hi();
    say_hi();
}
```

Figure 11-12. Program Sending Floating-Point Values to Function Declared Int

```
#include <stdio.h>

int add(a,b)
int a,b;
{
    int c;

    c = a + b;
    return c;
}

main()
{
    int a;

    a = add(3.0,4.0);
    printf("The value of 'a' is %d\n",a);
}
```

Figure 11-13. Results of Running Program

```
The value of 'a' is 0
```

```
Press any key to return to Turbo C. . .
```

The results are somewhat unexpected. Parameter types in function calls and function declarations must match. C will not normally warn you if such a problem exists. This may seem like a major flaw in the language. It would be a major flaw, if it weren't for function prototypes.

Prototypes

A prototype shows *Turbo C* the format for a function. *Turbo C* will use the prototype to make sure all values are converted to the proper type before the call is made. A prototype looks just like a function declaration except that all parameters are replaced with the appropriate types:

```
type function_name(type,type,type,. . .);
```

Note that unlike a declaration, the prototype ends with a semicolon. The prototype for add( ) looks like this:

```
int add(int,int);
```

In other words, it takes two int parameters and returns a single int. Try adding this prototype to the program in Figure 11-12 as shown in Figure 11-14. Now when you run this program, it works (see Figure 11-15).

Figure 11-14. Revised Program with Prototype

```
#include <stdio.h>

int add(int,int);

int add(a,b)
int a,b;
{
     int c;

     c = a + b;
     return c;
}

main()
{
     int a;

     a = add(3.0,4.0);
     printf("The value of 'a' is %d\n",a);
}
```

Figure 11-15. Results of Corrected Program

```
The value of 'a' is 7
```

```
Press any key to return to Turbo C. . .
```

Without a prototype, the main program does not know the types of the first two parameters in add( ). When the prototype is added, C can determine what types these parameters are and can therefore convert these values to the correct type.

As you know, some functions will not have any parameters. In order to create a prototype for a function that uses no parameters, you must use the keyword void. Follow the example in Figure 11-14. Just below the include directive and above the line *say_hi( )*, insert the line

void say_hi(void);

That will inform C that it is not expected to return a value when this function is called.

There is another feature of C that can be dangerous. The program will still compile even if you leave off the parentheses in a function. Try running the program in Figure 11-16. The function calls were ignored. Why? You may notice that some warning messages were produced (Figure 11-17).

Figure 11-16. Calling a Function Without Parentheses

```
#include <stdio.h>

say_hi()
{
        printf("Hi there!\n");
        printf("This was written in a function\n");
}

main()
{
     printf("Call it once:\n");

     say_hi;

     printf("Call it a couple more times\n");

     say_hi;
     say_hi;
}
```

Figure 11-17. Warning Messages Resulting from Program in Figure 11-16

```
     File      Edit      Run      Compile      Project      Options      Debug
                              ───────────── Edit ─────────────
       Line 13    Col 16   Insert Indent Tab  C:PROG11_5.C
 }

 main()
 {
         printf("Call it once:\n");

         say_hi;

         printf("Call it a couple more times\n");

         say_hi;
         say_hi;
 }
                                   ════════ Message ════════
 Compiling C:\TURBOC\PROG11_5.C:
 Warning C:\TURBOC\PROG11_5.C 13: Code has no effect in function main
 Warning C:\TURBOC\PROG11_5.C 17: Code has no effect in function main
 Warning C:\TURBOC\PROG11_5.C 18: Code has no effect in function main
 Linking PROG11_5.EXE:

 F1-Help  F5-Zoom  F6-Edit  F7/F8-Prev/Next error  F9-Make  F10-Main Menu
```

The three lines that contain the function calls are marked
as *code has no effect in function main.*

Every function is located at a certain place in memory.
This location is known as its *address*. There are two different
ways that you may use a function. You may call it, causing
the code it contains to be executed, or you may determine its
address. By including parentheses after the function name,
you're telling *Turbo C* that you want to call the function. By
leaving the parentheses off, you inform *Turbo C* that you want
the address of the function. If the parentheses are missing, it
assumes that you want to assign the address of the function to
something. Because there were no assignments, the warning
messages were produced.

If you're curious, you might want to try assigning this
value to a variable. Unfortunately, addresses are not integers
or floats, so they may not be stored in any variable that
you've learned how to declare. Later on, you'll learn about
new variable types that allow this.

Nesting Functions

Functions may be called from within other functions. Figure
11-18 contains an example of an add( ) function that calls a
second function to wait for a keypress.

Figure 11-18. Function that Calls Another Function

```
#include <stdio.h>

int add(int,int);


add(a,b)
int a,b;
{
        int c;

        c = a + b;
        return c;
}


main()
{
        int x,y;

        for(y=0;y<10;y++)
        {
                x = add(4,y);
                printf("The result is %d\n",x);
        }

}
```

First, notice that even though the function add( ) uses the
function pause( ), pause( ) is defined after add( ) in the file. Because *Turbo C* has seen the function prototype for pause( ),
which is

void pause(void);

and it knows the correct parameter types to use, it does not
need to know what the function pause( ) does as it compiles
add( ).

The second thing to notice is that the prototypes for add( )
and pause( ) are located at the beginning of the file. Placing
your prototypes at the beginning of your program is good programming practice for two reasons. As previously mentioned,

prototypes allow a function to be called from another function before it has been explicitly defined. Also, it helps keep programs organized if all prototypes are defined in one place. If your program is large, this can be especially helpful.

Finally, notice that the calls to add( ) use both values and variables. Until now, all function calls were given values as parameters. This is not required. A variable can be used in place of any number. This gives functions even more flexibility as evidenced by Figure 11-19. This program will add the number 4 to all values of y between 0 and 9.

Figure 11-19. Program Mixing Values and Variables

```
#include <stdio.h>

int add(int,int);
void pause(void);

add(a,b)
int a,b;
{
        int c;
        printf("Going to add %d and %d\n",a,b);
        pause();
        c = a + b;
        return c;
}

void pause(void)
{
        printf("Hit any key to continue\n");
        getch();
}

main()
{
        int x,y;
        y = 5;
        x = add(4,y);
        printf("The result is %d\n",x);
}
```

Global Variables

In previous examples, all variables used were local variables known only to the functions in which they were declared. It's possible to declare global variables visible to all functions that make up a program. To do this, simply declare the variable outside of any function declaration as in Figure 11-20.

Figure 11-20. Program with Global Variable *a*

```
#include <stdio.h>

int a;

main()
{
    a = 10;
    printf("a is %d\n",a);
}
```

The results of running this program will be identical to a similar program with *a* declared locally. Now use this variable in a second function (Figure 11-21).

Figure 11-21. Using Variable *a* in a Second Function

```
#include <stdio.h>

void print_it(void);

int a;

void print_it(void)
{

        printf("a is %d\n",a);
}

main()
{
        a = 10;
        print_it();
}
```

When you run this program, the results will be the same as in Figure 11-20. The variable *a* that was assigned the value 10 in main( ) is the same variable *a* in the function print_it( ). What if you had declared the variable *a* inside one of the functions instead? Run the program in Figure 11-22.

Figure 11-22. Declaring *a* from Within a Function

```
#include <stdio.h>

void print_it(void);


void print_it(void)
{
        int a;
        printf("a is %d\n",a);
}

main()
{
        a = 10;
        print_it();
}
```

This program won't compile because the variable *a* declared in the function print_it( ) cannot be seen by the function main( ). Main( ) considers *a* to be an undeclared variable. Can you fix this by declaring *a* in main( ) also? Run the program in Figure 11-23.

Figure 11-23. Declaring *a* in Two Functions

```
#include <stdio.h>

void print_it(void);

void print_it(void)
{
        int a;
        printf("a is %d\n",a);
}

main()
{
        int a;
        a = 10;
        print_it();
}
```

As you probably guessed, this still won't work. The variable *a* in main( ) is not the same variable as the *a* in print_it( ). The only way to allow both print_it( ) and main( ) access to the same variable is to declare it globally, outside of any function.

Global variables can be useful for sending information between procedures. They can also be very dangerous. The reason that functions have parameters is to centralize all information flow between a program and a function. Often you'll be tempted to use global variables to communicate between functions. This will work, but it makes your routines less portable. If you write a function that only uses parameters, it is usually a simple matter to include it in another program. This can save you much time and effort as you don't need to rewrite a useful function for every program that you wish to include it in.

If a function uses global variables, it becomes much harder to include. Without reading through the entire text, it is difficult to tell what global variables are used by which functions. If the program is long, you'll often have trouble telling the local variables from the global ones. Because any program that uses such a function will also have to have the same global declarations, such programs will have to be modified before they can use the function. Later on, when you learn how to break programs into separate files, this will become even more important.

Summary

In this chapter, you've learned how to declare and construct functions. You've learned the difference between a local variable (declared within a function) and a global variable (declared outside of any function). You now know how to pass values to a function through parameters and how to use a return statement to send values back to the calling function. You've learned that there is a void type variable which contains nothing at all. You've seen how to use prototypes to inform C of the kinds of variables to expect when a function is called and how to nest functions.

Until now, the focus has been on the tiny individual parts of a C program. Functions are the first step into the larger world of C programming. They're the building blocks of the program itself.

Chapter 12
Advanced Editing

Now that you've had time to familiarize yourself with the simpler editing commands, this chapter will present some more powerful commands. The first set of commands are known collectively as block commands. These commands allow you to delete, copy, or move large sections of text. The second set of commands involve searching for and replacing text strings.

Block Commands

The following commands are called block commands because they operate on blocks of text. A block of text is defined as any piece of text that has been marked with block-mark commands.

For the sake of the demonstrations in this chapter, type the following text into the Edit window:

This is the first paragraph. This is going to
be moved around the file.

This is the second paragraph. A copy will be
made and the original deleted.

This is the third paragraph. Its purpose is merely to exist,
to take up space, to serve as a marker.

This is the fourth paragraph. Its sole purpose
is to make the screen look more full.

This file also contains some random text.
This will be used to demonstrate the search commands.

This file contains a number of things for Turbo
C to look for. In fact "look for" is one of these things.

All block-editing commands consist of two keystrokes beginning with Ctrl-K. When you type a Ctrl-K the characters ^K will appear in the upper left corner of the screen as in Figure 12-1.

Figure 12-1. ˆK Symbol in Upper Left Screen Indicates That the Editor is Awaiting Additional Keystroke

```
   File      Edit      Run     Compile   Project    Options    Debug
                              ===== Edit =====
 ˆK     Line 1      Col 1     Insert Indent Tab  C:NONAME.C




                         ------- Message -------



```
F1-Help F5-Zoom F6-Message F9-Make F10-Main menu

This lets you know that the *Turbo C* editor is preparing to do a block command. Your next keystroke will tell *Turbo C* which command to execute. The Ctrl-K,B key sequence marks the beginning of a block (Figure 12-2).

Figure 12-2. Ctrl-K,B Key Sequence Marks Beginning of Block

```
   File      Edit      Run     Compile   Project    Options    Debug
                              ===== Edit =====
        Line 15     Col 5    Insert Indent Tab  C:BLOCK.C
 This is the first paragraph.  This is going to
 be moved around the file.

 This is the second paragraph.  A copy will be
 made and the original deleted.

 This is the third paragraph. Its purpose is merely to exist,
 to take up space, to serve as a marker.


 This is the fourth paragraph. Its sole purpose
 is to make the screen look more full.
                         ------- Message -------


```
F1-Help F5-Zoom F6-Message F9-Make F10-Main menu

Move to the beginning of the second paragraph and type Ctrl-K. Notice that ^K appears at the upper left corner of the screen. Now type the letter *B*. You've just marked the beginning of the block.

Nothing will appear on the screen. The beginning and ending points are invisible until they have both been marked. You must now position the end of the mark. This can be done with the Ctrl-K,K key sequence. Move to the end of the second paragraph and press Ctrl-K and then the letter *K*. This will cause all text between the two marks to be highlighted (Figure 12-3).

Figure 12-3. Highlighted Text

```
   File     Edit     Run     Compile    Project    Options    Debug
                           ══════ Edit ══════
     Line 5      Col 34   Insert Indent Tab C:BLOCK.C
  This is the first paragraph.  This is going to
  be moved around the file.

  This is the second paragraph.  A copy will be
  made and the original deleted.

  This is the third paragraph. Its purpose is merely to exist,
  to take up space, to serve as a marker.


  This is the fourth paragraph. Its sole purpose
  is to make the screen look more full.
  ─────────────────────── Message ───────────────────────




  ────────────────────────────────────────────────────────
  F1-Help  F5-Zoom  F6-Message  F9-Make  F10-Main menu
```

There are three important things that you can do with a block of text.

• You can move it around in the file.
• You can make copies of it.
• You can remove it entirely.

Copying a block of text is a simple action once you've marked the block. Move the cursor to a position just prior to the first paragraph (Figure 12-4).

Figure 12-4. Move Cursor to Position Before First Paragraph

```
    File      Edit      Run     Compile     Project     Options     Debug
                              == Edit ==
      Line 1      Col 4    Insert Indent Tab C:BLOCK.C

This is the first paragraph.  This is going to
be moved around the file.

This is the second paragraph.  A copy will be
made and the original deleted.

This is the third paragraph. Its purpose is merely to exist,
to take up space, to serve as a marker.

This is the fourth paragraph. Its sole purpose
                          == Message ==




F1-Help  F5-Zoom  F6-Message  F9-Make  F10-Main menu
```

The Ctrl-K,C key sequence will copy a marked block to the cursor position. Type Ctrl-K,C. There will now be two copies of the second paragraph—one before the first paragraph and one after. The copy that was just created will be highlighted. This is now the new marked block (Figure 12-5).

Figure 12-5. Copied Block Is Now Marked

```
    File      Edit      Run     Compile     Project     Options     Debug
                              == Edit ==
      Line 1      Col 1    Insert Indent Tab C:BLOCK.C
This is the second paragraph.  A copy will be
made and the original deleted.

This is the first paragraph.  This is going to
be moved around the file.

This is the second paragraph.  A copy will be
made and the original deleted.

This is the third paragraph. Its purpose is merely to exist,
to take up space, to serve as a marker.

This is the fourth paragraph. Its sole purpose
                          == Message ==




F1-Help  F5-Zoom  F6-Message  F9-Make  F10-Main menu
```

You may also move a block. This is similar to copying a block except that the original block is deleted after it is copied. Mark the original first paragraph with Ctrl-K,B at the beginning and Ctrl-K,K at the end. Once this block is marked, move the cursor to the end of the file and type Ctrl-K,V. This will move the marked text to the place where the cursor is located (Figure 12-6).

Figure 12-6. Block Moved from Middle to End of Text

```
     File      Edit      Run     Compile      Project     Options      Debug
                                ═══ Edit ═══
  ┌─────────────────────────────────────────────────────────────────────────┐
  │     Line 15    Col 1    Insert Indent Tab C:BLOCK.C                       │
  │This is the second paragraph.  A copy will be                              │
  │made and the original deleted.                                            │
  │                                                                           │
  │This is the third paragraph. Its purpose is merely to exist,               │
  │to take up space, to serve as a marker.                                    │
  │                                                                           │
  │This is the fourth paragraph. Its sole purpose                             │
  │                                                                           │
  │This is the first paragraph.  This is going to                             │
  │be moved around the file.                                                  │
  │                                                                           │
  │                                                                           │
  ├──────────────────────────── Message ─────────────────────────────────────┤
  │                                                                           │
  │                                                                           │
  │                                                                           │
  │                                                                           │
  └─────────────────────────────────────────────────────────────────────────┘
  F1-Help  F5-Zoom  F6-Message  F9-Make  F10-Main menu
```

You may also remove a block with Ctrl-K,Y. Mark the paragraph that you copied earlier. Type Ctrl-K,Y. This will remove the paragraph. There will now be no marked text (Figure 12-7).

Figure 12-7. Paragraph Removed from Middle of Text

```
     File      Edit      Run     Compile      Project     Options      Debug
                                ═══ Edit ═══
  ┌─────────────────────────────────────────────────────────────────────────┐
  │     Line 3     Col 1    Insert Indent Tab C:BLOCK.C                       │
  │This is the second paragraph.  A copy will be                              │
  │made and the original deleted.                                            │
  │                                                                           │
  │                                                                           │
  │This is the third paragraph. Its purpose is merely to exist,               │
  │to take up space, to serve as a marker.                                    │
  │This is the fourth paragraph. Its sole purpose                             │
  │is to make the screen look full.                                           │
  ├──────────────────────────── Message ─────────────────────────────────────┤
  │                                                                           │
  │                                                                           │
  │                                                                           │
  └─────────────────────────────────────────────────────────────────────────┘
  F1-Help  F5-Zoom  F6-Message  F9-Make  F10-Main menu
```

Marked text will never affect your program in any way. You may compile a program with marked blocks with no difficulty. The only reason for having marked text is to use the block-edit commands.

Marks are only valid for the current editing session. If you save a file with marks in it, you'll discover that the marks have disappeared when you look at the file later.

Searching

The search commands allow you to find a certain word or sequence of characters in a file. You can use them simply to find a section of your program or to quickly replace all occurrences of a word (or series of characters) with another.

To search through a file for a string of letters, you must use the Ctrl-Q,F command. (Ctrl-Q invokes the quick cursor-movement commands just as Ctrl-K invoked the block commands.) Move the cursor to the beginning of the file with Ctrl-Q,R. When the cursor is at the beginning, type Ctrl-Q,F. In the upper left corner of the screen, the word *Find:* will appear (Figure 12-8).

Figure 12-8. *Find:* Appears in Upper Left Corner

```
     File     Edit     Run     Compile    Project    Options    Debug
                                 ═══ Edit ═══
 Find:
 This is the second paragraph.  A copy will be
 made and the original deleted.

 This is the third paragraph. Its purpose is merely to exist,
 to take up space, to serve as a marker.

 This is the fourth paragraph. Its sole purpose
 is to make the screen look more full.

 This is the first paragraph.  This is going to
 be moved around the file.

 This file also contains some random text.
                          ═══ Message ═══


 F1-Help  F5-Zoom  F6-Message  F9-Make  F10-Main menu
```

Turbo C is asking you for a search string. Enter the words *look for* at this prompt and press Enter. *Turbo C* will then prompt you with the word *options*. There are a number of different ways that *Turbo C* can search. The options prompt allows you to choose between these methods. Press Enter to choose the most basic search (Figure 12-9). Other options will be explained later. Soon after you do this, the cursor will move to the first occurrence of the string *look for* in the file (Figure 12-10).

Figure 12-9. Leave Option Blank to Choose Basic Search

```
    File      Edit      Run     Compile    Project    Options    Debug
                              ═════ Edit ═════
Options:
This is the second paragraph.  A copy will be
made and the original deleted.

This is the third paragraph. Its purpose is merely to exist,
to take up space, to serve as a marker.

This is the fourth paragraph. Its sole purpose
is to make the screen look more full.

This is the first paragraph.  This is going to
be moved around the file.

This file also contains some random text.
                           ─────── Message ───────




F1-Help  F5-Zoom  F6-Message  F9-Make  F10-Main menu
```

Figure 12-10. Results of Search for the String *look for*

```
    File      Edit      Run     Compile    Project    Options    Debug
                              ═════ Edit ═════
      Line 16    Col 54   Insert Indent Tab C:BLOCK.C
to take up space, to serve as a marker.

This is the fourth paragraph. Its sole purpose
is to make the screen look more full.

This is the first paragraph.  This is going to
be moved around the file.

This file also contains some random text.
This will be used to demonstrate the search commands.
This file contains a number of things for Turbo
C to look for.  In fact, "look for" is one of these things.
                           ─────── Message ───────




F1-Help  F5-Zoom  F6-Message  F9-Make  F10-Main menu
```

Once a string has been found, you may search for further occurrences of this string by typing Ctrl-L. Try this now (Figure 12-11). The cursor will now be pointing to the second occurrence of the search string *(look for)*.

Figure 12-11. Cursor Points to Second Occurrence of Text String

```
     File    Edit    Run    Compile    Project    Options    Debug
═══════════════════════════════ Edit ══════════════════════════════
    Line 16    Col 54  Insert Indent Tab C:BLOCK.C
to take up space, to serve as a marker.

This is the fourth paragraph. Its sole purpose
is to make the screen look more full.

This is the first paragraph.  This is going to
be moved around the file.

This file also contains some random text.
This will be used to demonstrate the search commands.
This file contains a number of things for Turbo
C to look for.  In fact, "look for" is one of these things.
─────────────────────────── Message ───────────────────────────




F1-Help  F5-Zoom  F6-Message  F9-Make  F10-Main menu
```

Ctrl-L may be used at any time during the editing process. Move the cursor back to the beginning of the file and type Ctrl-L. The cursor should again move to the first occurrence of the words *look for*. Typing Ctrl-L again will move to the second occurrence. Move to the beginning and enter some more text. Press Ctrl-L again. This will still find the appropriate words.

Now search for the string *something else* by typing Ctrl-Q,F and entering *something else* at the prompt. Again, press Enter at the options prompt. *Turbo C* will respond with a *Search string not found* message. *Turbo C* always begins its search from the current cursor location. Move the cursor past the second occurrence of *look for* and search for this string using Ctrl-Q,F. *Turbo C* will again respond with *Search string not found* (Figure 12-12).

Figure 12-12. Unable to Find Search String; Editor Responds with *Search string not found*

```
    File      Edit      Run     Compile    Project    Options    Debug
============================== Edit ==============================
Search string not found. Press <ESC>
    to take up space, to serve as a marker.

    This is the fourth paragraph.  Its sole purpose
    is to make the screen look more full.

    This is the first paragraph.  This is going to
    be moved around the file.

    This file also contains some random text
    that will be used to demonstrate the search commands
    This file contains a number of things for Turbo
    C to look for.  In fact, "look for" is one of these things.
------------------------------ Message ---------------------------




------------------------------------------------------------------
  F1-Help  F5-Zoom  F6-Message  F9-Make  F10-Main menu
```

Now type Ctrl-L again. *Turbo C* will again say *Search string not found*. Ctrl-L always repeats the most recent search command whether it was successful or not.

Replacing Text

The keypress sequence to initiate a search-and-replace action is Ctrl-Q,A. This editing command works in a manner similar to Ctrl-Q,F (search) except that it can substitute a replacement string for the search string. Move to the top of the file and type Ctrl-Q,A. You'll again be asked for a search string (Figure 12-13).

Figure 12-13. *Find:* Prompt for Search String

```
    File      Edit      Run     Compile    Project    Options    Debug
============================== Edit ==============================
Find:
This is the second paragraph.  A copy will be
made and the original deleted.

This is the third paragraph. Its purpose is merely to exist,
to take up space, to serve as a marker.

This is the fourth paragraph. Its sole purpose
is to make the screen look more full.

This is the first paragraph.  This is going to
be moved around the file.

This file also contains some random text.
------------------------------ Message ---------------------------




------------------------------------------------------------------
  F1-Help  F5-Zoom  F6-Message  F9-Make  F10-Main menu
```

Enter the words *look for*. When you press Enter you'll be given a second prompt asking for a replacement string. Type *found it!* and press Enter (Figure 12-14).

Figure 12-14. Enter Replacement String at Prompt

```
     File      Edit      Run      Compile    Project     Options     Debug
                             ══════ Edit ═════════════════════════════════════
 Replace with: found it!▓▓▓
 This is the second paragraph.   a copy will be
 made & the original deleted.

 This is the third paragraph. Its purpose is merely to exist,
 to take up space, to serve as a marker.

 This is the fourth paragraph. Its sole purpose
 is to make the screen look more full.

 This is the first paragraph.   This is going to
 be moved around the file.

 This file also contains some random text.
 ├────────────────────────────── Message ──────────────────────────────────┤




 F1-Help  F5-Zoom  F6-Message  F9-Make  F10-Main menu
```

You'll again be asked for options. Press Enter to choose the most basic search and replace. The cursor will again move to the first occurrence of *look for*. This time, however, the words *replace (Y/N)* will appear in the upper left corner of the Edit window. *Turbo C* is asking you whether or not you'd like to replace the string with the replacement string. Type the letter *Y* (Figure 12-15).

Figure 12-15. The String *look for* Is Changed to *found it!*

```
     File      Edit      Run      Compile    Project     Options     Debug
                             ══════ Edit ═════════════════════════════════════
     Line 16    Col 15   Insert Indent Tab C:BLOCK.C
 to take up space, to serve as a marker.

 This is the fourth paragraph. Its sole purpose
 is to make the screen look more full.

 This is the first paragraph.   This is going to
 be moved around the file.

 This file also contains some random text.
 This will be used to demonstrate the search commands.
 This file contains a number of things for Turbo
 C to found it!.  In fact, "look for" is one of these things.
 ├────────────────────────────── Message ──────────────────────────────────┤




 F1-Help  F5-Zoom  F6-Message  F9-Make  F10-Main menu
```

You'll notice that the first occurrence of the string *look for* has been replaced with the string *found it!*. Try typing Ctrl-L. The cursor will move to the second occurrence of the search string (Figure 12-16).

Figure 12-16. Ctrl-L Moves to Next Occurrence of String

```
    File      Edit      Run      Compile      Project    Options    Debug
                                  ═══════ Edit ═══════
 ┌─────────────────────────────────────────────────────────────────────────┐
 │Replace (Y/N):                                                             │
 │to take up space, to serve as a marker.                                    │
 │                                                                           │
 │This is the fourth paragraph. Its sole purpose                             │
 │is to make the screen look more full.                                      │
 │                                                                           │
 │This is the first paragraph.  This is going to                             │
 │be moved around the file.                                                  │
 │                                                                           │
 │This file also contains some random text.                                  │
 │This will be used to demonstrate the search commands.                      │
 │This file contains a number of things for Turbo                            │
 │C to found it!.  In fact, "look for" is one of these things.               │
 │                                ─── Message ───                            │
 │                                                                           │
 │                                                                           │
 │                                                                           │
 │                                                                           │
 └─────────────────────────────────────────────────────────────────────────┘
    F1-Help  F5-Zoom  F6-Message  F9-Make  F10-Main menu
```

This time, type the letter *N*. The string is not replaced.

Search Options

Search options allow you to do a number of useful things. Suppose you had to change every occurrence of a variable name to something else. With the commands you've seen so far, this would be tedious in a long program. You'd have to use Ctrl-L to look for each occurrence and then answer Y to replace the prompt. Certain options allow you to avoid this inconvenience.

Replace all occurrences. The G option allows you to replace all occurrences throughout the entire file. You'll still be asked whether the text should be replaced for each occurrence, but you won't need to type the Ctrl-L. Try replacing every occurrence of *and* with *&*. Type Ctrl-Q,A. When it prompts for the search string with *Find:* type *and*. When the *replace with:* prompt for the replacement string appears, type *&*. When the *options:* prompt appears, type the letter *G* and press Enter (Figure 12-17).

Chapter 12

Figure 12-17. Enter *G* at Option Prompt to Replace All Occurrences

```
    File      Edit      Run      Compile    Project    Options    Debug
                                  ===== Edit =====
 Options: G
 This is the second paragraph.  a copy will be
 made & the original deleted.

 This is the third paragraph. Its purpose is merely to exist,
 to take up space, to serve as a marker.

 This is the fourth paragraph. Its sole purpose
 is to make the screen look more full.

 This is the first paragraph.  This is going to
 be moved around the file.

 This file also contains some random text.
                            ===== Message =====




```

F1-Help F5-Zoom F6-Message F9-Make F10-Main menu

Turbo C will automatically jump to each occurrence of *and* in the file and ask whether it should be replaced.

Replace all occurrences without permission. The N option will cause *Turbo C* to replace all occurrences without prompting you for permission to do so. Try replacing every occurrence of the lowercase letter *a* with uppercase *A*. This time, when it asks for options, type both the letters *G* and *N*. This will cause the search to find all occurrences (as in the previous example) and will also suppress the question (Figure 12-18).

Figure 12-18. *GN* Option Replaces All Occurrences Without Permission

```
    File      Edit      Run      Compile    Project    Options    Debug
                                  ===== Edit =====
 Options: GN
 This is the second paragraph.  a copy will be
 made & the original deleted.

 This is the third paragraph. Its purpose is merely to exist,
 to take up space, to serve as a marker.

 This is the fourth paragraph. Its sole purpose
 is to make the screen look more full.

 This is the first paragraph.  This is going to
 be moved around the file.

 This file also contains some random text.
                            ===== Message =====




```

F1-Help F5-Zoom F6-Message F9-Make F10-Main menu

162

This time, no questions were asked. Instead *Turbo C* replaced each occurrence it found. With this option, *Turbo C* will not show you everything it replaces. *Turbo C* will pause as it searches through the file. When the brief pause is over, all occurrences of the lowercase letter *a* will be replaced with uppercase *A*.

Summary
During the course of this chapter, you've learned to copy, move, and delete large blocks of marked text. You should also now know how to search for and replace text strings. This chapter has shown you how to search and replace on both a case-by-case basis and globally.

These advanced editing commands can be a great boon to the programmer. The block text commands allow you to copy large amounts of text. This can save programming time when a large number of similar pieces of code must be written. Instead of typing every copy, merely enter the text once, copy it, and then make any necessary changes to each copy. Later in this book, you'll see some examples where this editing feature saves a great deal of time.

The search commands can be useful both in moving quickly through your program and in fixing errors. A common programming error is to give a variable two different names (*sum_of_interest* and *interest_sum*, for example). Suppose the variable name appeared in fifty different places. Making the names agree will take a large amount of effort and time. Even when you are through, you have no way of knowing that you found all occurrences of the incorrect string. The search-and-replace commands will allow you to fix such an error with a single command.

Section Four
Advanced C

Chapter 13
Projects

C allows you to separate a program into a number of different files. Splitting programs into more manageable pieces has a number of advantages especially if the program is large.

Object Files
When a program is compiled, *Turbo C* only needs to compile those files in which changes have been made. During compilation, *Turbo C* creates a new file called an *object file* for each text file.

An object file contains a machine language translation of a C text file. If a text file has not been changed, *Turbo C* doesn't have to translate it again. If your entire program is contained in a single file, this capability doesn't make much difference. Making a single change will force *Turbo C* to re-translate the entire program, even if only a single line was changed.

If your program were separated into a number of files, *Turbo C* would only have to recompile the file in which the change was made. Thus breaking up a large file into several smaller portions will save you a tremendous amount of compilation time.

Common Functions
The other major advantage of splitting a program into separate files is that you may write a number of different programs that share common functions. Suppose that you were impressed with the function add( ) in the previous chapter and wanted to use it in all of your programs. Because of the way C operates, you wouldn't have to rewrite this function each time you write a program. Every program could include the file that contains add( ).

Rules for Splitting Programs

There are a few rules for splitting programs apart, but they are all fairly straightforward. If the program has no global variables, then this task is even simpler. The smallest unit of executable code that can be separated is a single function.

In addition, the prototype for a function must appear in every file in which that function is either called or declared. Because function prototypes are often used in all files that make up a particular program, they are often placed in special header files and loaded using the include directive. As you may have guessed, this is the purpose of stdio.h. This file contains prototypes for all of the standard functions such as printf( ), scanf( ), and getch( ). A program split into smaller parts would look something like the diagram in Figure 13-1.

Figure 13-1. Diagram of Program

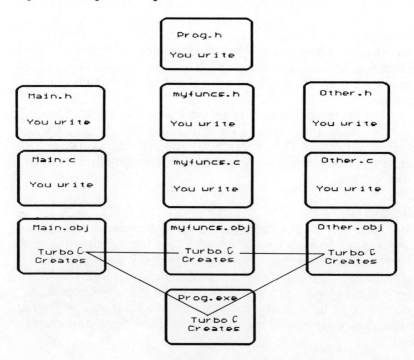

Figure 13-1 depicts a program that has been split into three files. The first file contains the prototypes for all functions in the program. Create the file in Figure 13-2 and save it under the name my_prog.h.

Figure 13-2. my_prog.h

```
/* my_prog.h */

void pause(void);
void print_number(int);
int get_number(void);
```

Figure 13-3 contains a pause routine that you'll probably want to use in a number of programs. Using the *Turbo C* editor, enter the function as shown in the figure and save it under the name pause.c.

Figure 13-3. pause.c

```
/* pause.c */
#include <stdio.h>
#include "my_prog.h"          /* Read in the prototypes */

void pause()
{
        printf("<Hit any key to continue>\n");
        getch();
}
```

The file in Figure 13-4 contains the major functions used with your program. Enter these functions in the editor and save the file under the name my_funcs.c.

Figure 13-4. my_funcs.c

```
/* my_funcs.c */
#include <stdio.h>
#include "my_prog.c"

int number;

void print_number()
{
        printf("The number is %d\n",number);
}

int get_number()
{
        int a;

        do
        {
                printf("Enter a number between 1 and 10:");
                scanf("%d",&a);
        }
        while(a < 1 || a > 10);  /* must be between 1 and 10 */
        return a;
}
```

The file in Figure 13-5 contains the main program. Enter this into the *Turbo C* editor and save it as my_prog.c.

Figure 13-5. my_prog.c

```
/* my_prog.c */
#include <stdio.h>
#include "my_prog.h"

main()
{
            extern int number;

            number=get_number();
            print_number();
            pause();
}
```

Project Files

A project file tells *Turbo C* how to create a program. It consists of a list of files that make up that program. *Turbo C* uses this file to find all parts of a program during compilation. A project file is necessary to compile any program made up of more than one file. Enter the editor one final time and enter the names of all of the C files (Figure 13-6).

Figure 13-6. my_prog.prj

```
my_prog.c
my_funcs.c
pause.c
```

Now save this file under the name my_prog.prj. You now have written all the text necessary for your project. You now need to tell *Turbo C* which project to compile. You can do this by selecting Project on the main menu or by typing Alt-P. A menu will pop up. Choose the first option, *Project Name* (Figure 13-7).

Figure 13-7. Select *Project Name*

```
   File      Edit      Run      Compile      Project      Options      Debug
                                 Edit
     Line 1      Col 1    Insert Indent Ta  Project name
/* my_funcs.c */                               Project Name
#include <stdio.h>                            *.PRJ
#include "my_prog.h"

int number;

void print_number()
{
        printf("The number is %d\n",number);
}

int get_number()
{                                  Message



```

F1-Help Esc-Abort

In this window, enter the name my_prog.prj and return. Now type Alt-R to run your program. The *Turbo C* compiler will then compile all three of your files, link them together, and run the resulting program. (See Figure 13-8.)

Figure 13-8. Results of Running Program

```
Enter a number between 1 and 10:653
Enter a number between 1 and 10:4521
Enter a number between 1 and 10:43
Enter a number between 1 and 10:-636
Enter a number between 1 and 10:42
Enter a number between 1 and 10:6
The number is 6
<Hit any key to continue>
```

From now on, you may edit and run this program just as you would any other. It doesn't matter which file you're currently editing, typing Alt-R will compile and run the entire program. Try making a change in one of your files. For example, change the read routine by adding a pause( ) function call as shown in Figure 13-9.

Figure 13-9. Changed Read Routine

```
int get_number()
{
        int a;

        do
        {
                printf("Enter a number between 1 and 10:");
                scanf("%d",&a);
        }
        while(a < 1 || a > 10);  /* must be between 1 and 10 */
        return a;
}
```

Now type Alt-R again. Notice that only the file named my_funcs.c is recompiled.

You might think that errors would be handled differently when a file is split into pieces. This is not the case. In each of your three files, place the string *bad command* at some arbitrary place and press Alt-R. *Turbo C* will catch all three errors. Even though they are in separate files, *Turbo C* has no trouble moving between them. The only exception occurs when you're about to leave a file by pressing F7 or F8. In this case, a new box may appear as shown in Figure 13-10.

Figure 13-10. Verify Box

```
   File    Edit    Run    Compile   Project    Options    Debug
===================================== Edit ========================
    Line 8     Col 12   Insert Indent Tab C:PAUSE.C
#include <stdio.h>
#include "my_prog.h"                    /* Read in the prototypes
*/                 === Verify ===
           | PAUSE.C not saved.   Save? (Y/N) |
void paus  ====================================
{
bad command
                printf("<Hit any key to continue>");
                getch();
}


================================= Message ==========================
 Compiling C:\TURBOC\PAUSE.C:
 Error C:\TURBOC\PAUSE.C 8: Undefined symbol 'bad' in function pause
 Warning C:\TURBOC\PAUSE.C 8: Code has no effect in function pause
 Error C:\TURBOC\PAUSE.C 8: Statement missing ; in function pause

F1-Help  Esc-Abort
```

This box prevents you from forgetting to save files as you work on them. Also, if enough errors occur in one file, *Turbo C* will not attempt to compile another file.

Global Variables

Global variables can be tricky when you're dealing with multiple files. Modify print—number( ) (shown in Figure 13-4) to print a global variable *number* instead of the parameter *a*. Remember to change the prototype in my—prog.h to *void print—number(void)*. You should also change the function print—number in my—funcs.c as in Figure 13-12.

Figure 13-11. Main Function Declaring a Global Variable

```
/* my_prog.c */
#include <stdio.h>
#include "my_progs.h"

int number;

main()
{
        number=get_number();
        print_number();
        pause();
}
```

You'll now need to change the main file so that *number* is global as in Figure 13-11. What happens when this is compiled? An error message appears (Figure 13-12).

Figure 13-12. Error Message

```
    File     Edit      Run      Compile     Project      Options      Debug
                                     Edit
      Line 7      Col 43   Insert Indent Tab C:MY_FUNCS.C
/* my_funcs.c */
#include <stdio.h>
#include "my_prog.h"

void print_number()
{
        printf("The number is %d\n",number);
}

int get_number()
{
        int a;

                                     Message
 Compiling C:\TURBOC\MY_FUNCS.C:
 Error C:\TURBOC\MY_FUNCS.C 7: Undefined symbol 'number' in function print_num
```

F1-Help F5-Zoom F6-Edit F7/F8-Prev/Next error F9-Make F10-Main Menu

You tried to use the variable *number* in the file named my_funcs.c. Unfortunately, that file knew nothing about that variable. Can this be fixed by placing this variable in my_funcs.c also? (See Figure 13-13.)

Figure 13-13. Declaring Global Variable in my_funcs.c

```
     File      Edit      Run    Compile   Project   Options    Debug
                                    Edit
     Line 1      Col 1    Insert Indent Tab C:MY_FUNCS.C
/* my_funcs.c */
#include <stdio.h>
#include "my_prog.h"

int number;

void print_number()
{
        printf("The number is %d\n",number);
}

int get_number()
{
                                 Message
  Compiling C:\TURBOC\PROGS\MY_PROG.C:
  Linking MY_PROG.EXE:
  Linker Error: _number defined in module MY_PROG.C is duplicated in module MY_
```

F1-Help F5-Zoom F6-Edit F7/F8-Prev/Next error F9-Make F10-Main Menu

If you compile the program now, the compiler will tell you that the variable is declared twice.

What you have to do is to declare the variable once—in my_prog.c. Then, in every file that uses this variable, use a new declaration to declare the variable. This is the *extern* declaration. In the file my_funcs.c, replace the declaration of *number* with this declaration:

extern int number;

This statement tells C that there is an integer variable called *number* and that its location is external to this file. Run the program now. It should work as expected (see Figure 13-14).

The keyword extern can be placed before any legal variable declaration. It asserts that the declaration exists in another file and should be considered declared in the current file also.

As you can see, global variables can cause difficulties in large, multifile programs. There are times where you'll have to use such variables, but they should be avoided whenever possible.

The project utility is a very powerful feature of *Turbo C*. Projects allow you to handle large numbers of text files with little thought.

Figure 13-14. Results of Running Program

```
Enter a number between 1 and 10:3
The number is 3
<Hit any key to continue>
```

```
Press any key to return to Turbo C. . .
```

Summary

In this chapter, you learned the importance of breaking large programs down into component parts. This saves time when writing a program and when compiling it. You also learned the rules by which a program may be broken down. Header files containing prototypes should be constructed to inform C in advance of upcoming functions.

You also saw how to bind the constituent files together at compile time with a project file. You should now know how to declare and use a global variable by using an extern statement. You were also warned that global variables can be difficult to manage and should be avoided if possible.

Chapter 14
Arrays

A data structure is a collection of variables used to hold large amounts of data. The simplest data structure is the array. An array is a sequential list of variables of the same type, tied together under the same name. For example, say you have the numbers 10, 15, 12, and 21. These could be stored in an array of integers. Each number would be one element of the array. The number 10 would be element 0, 15 would be element 1, and so on. Notice that the array begins with element 0. The general syntax to declare an array is

type array_name[number_of_elements];

Such a declaration creates an array of the type specified and names it *array_name*. There are *number_of_elements* variables in the array. To access an element of the array, use the array name as you would a normal variable, followed by the element you wish to access in brackets:

array_name[element_number];

Figure 14-1 contains a simple example program that uses an array.

Figure 14-1. A Program Demonstrating Use of Arrays

```
#include <stdio.h>

main()
{
    int number_list[10];      /* an array of 10 integers */

    number_list[4] = 23;
    number_list[0] = 52;

    printf("Element %d is %d\n",4,number_list[4]);
    printf("Element %d is %d\n",0,number_list[0]);
}
```

This program creates an array of ten integers and names it *number_list*. These integers may be accessed using the array name followed by the element number in brackets—in this case, *number_list[0]* through *number_list[9]*.

It is important to remember that *number_list* itself is not a legal variable. The following statement is illegal and would cause a compiler error:

```
number_list = 51;
```

The real power of arrays lies in the fact that you may use variables to access an element in an array. In the previous example, an element was accessed with an integer constant:

```
number_list[4] = 23;
```

You can also access an element using a variable:

```
char i = 4;
number_list[i] = 23;
```

Suppose you wanted to store the squares of the first 20 integers. Without using a variable to access elements, you'd have to resort to the method shown in Figure 14-2.

Figure 14-2. Filling an Array Element by Element

```
square[1]  = 1*1;
square[2]  = 2*2;
square[3]  = 3*3;
square[4]  = 4*4;
square[5]  = 5*5;
square[6]  = 6*6;
square[7]  = 7*7;
square[8]  = 8*8;
square[9]  = 9*9;
square[10] = 10*10;
square[11] = 11*11;
square[12] = 12*12;
square[13] = 13*13;
square[14] = 14*14;
square[15] = 15*15;
square[16] = 16*16;
square[17] = 17*17;
square[18] = 18*18;
square[19] = 19*19;
square[20] = 20*20;
```

This is very inefficient. An array used inside a loop will reduce those 20 lines to just 2 lines. Figure 14-3 shows how this might be done.

Figure 14-3. Filling an Array with a *For* Loop

```
int i;
int square[21]; /* array of 20 square */

for(i=1;i<=20;i++)
        square[i] = i * i;
```

Figure 14-4 contains a program that more fully illustrates how arrays may be used.

Figure 14-4. A More Complex Program Using Arrays

```
#include <stdio.h>
#define TRUE -1
#define FALSE 0

main()
{
        int i;
        float results[10];

        printf("Please enter 10 real numbers\n");

        for(i=0;i<10;i++)
        {
                printf("Number %d:",i+1);
                scanf("%f",&results[i]);
        }

        printf("The numbers have now been entered\n");
        printf("Enter a number between 1 and 10 to see\n");
        printf("a result, 0 to quit\n");

        do
        {
                printf(":");
                scanf("%d",&i);
                if(i > 0 && i < 11)      /* a legal element (1-10) */
                printf("Element %d contains %f\n",i,results[i-1]);
                                         /* Elements range from 0 to 9 */
        }
        while(i != 0);
}
```

Run this program. You'll note that this program has two sections. The first section reads ten numbers into an array, and the second allows the user to look at any of these numbers.

The program illustrates a number of points. It shows how elements may be accessed inside two different kinds of loops. In the *for* loop, each element is accessed sequentially one at a time. In the *do* loop, elements are accessed according to user input. Also note the difference in type between the elements in the array and the type of the variable used to access those elements. The array is declared as type float. Whenever an element of the array is accessed, it must be treated as a float.

For any array, the variable used to identify the element within the array must be an integer. In other words, an array may be made up of any kind of value, but to specify which element within the array, you must use whole numbers. There is no array element 2.5, although element 2 may contain the value 2.5.

Finally, the program asks the user to enter a number between 1 and 10. Because all arrays start with element 0, this must be converted to an element number between 0 and 9. This is an easy thing to forget to do, and it can often cause errors that are very difficult to track. Try changing $i-1$ to i in this line from the previous example:

printf("Element %d contains %f\n",i,results[i−1]);

Run the program again. It seems to work. Now try to access element 10 (see Figure 14-5).

Figure 14-5. Trying to Access Element 10

```
Please enter 10 real numbers
Number 1:324
Number 2:5
Number 3:27623
Number 4:7
Number 5:23
Number 6:72
Number 7:5.55
Number 8:6.66
Number 9:737.77
Number 10:54
The numbers have now been entered
Enter a number between 1 and 10 to see
a result, 0 to quit
:9
Element 9 contains 54.000000
:4
Element 4 contains 23.000000
:5
Element 5 contains 72.000000
:10
Element 10 contains 0.000000
:
```

It seems to work for numbers between 1 and 9 because these numbers are legal element numbers. When you use the number 10, C looks for the nonexistent eleventh element. This is an undefined variable as only ten variables were declared.

Character Strings

Suppose you wanted to store a whole word or phrase in a variable. How would you do it? The obvious way would be to place such a phrase in an array of characters. This is done so often that such character arrays are given a special name. Any array declared as type char is called a string variable.

You already have some experience with strings. A string constant is simply a phrase surrounded by quotation marks:

"This is a string constant."

In some ways, string variables can be treated like variables of simpler types. For example, you may use scanf( ) to read a string variable and printf( ) to print a string variable (%s is the appropriate format specification.)

In other ways, string variables cannot be treated like variables of simpler types. As with any array, a string cannot be used with the assignment operator. To move a string from one character array to another, you must use the string copy function strcpy( ). This function has two parameters, the source string and the destination string:

char dest[80];
char source[80];
strcpy(dest, source);

Figure 14-6 contains a program that manipulates strings.

Figure 14-6. A Program that Manipulates Strings

```
#include <stdio.h>

main()
{
        char string1[80],string2[80]; /* two strings */

        printf("Please enter a string\n:");
        scanf("%s",string1);            /* read a string */

        printf("Moving this to string2\n");
        strcpy(string2,string1);

        printf("The string is %s\n",string2);
}
```

Notice that the & doesn't have to be used with a string as it does with most variables in scanf( ). In fact, this is true of all arrays.

Summary

Arrays are not difficult to understand. An array is simply a group of variables tied together under a common name. Each member of the array is called an element. The number used to refer to an element must be a whole, positive number, but the contents of that element may be a value of any type, as specified when the array is declared.

Strings are arrays of characters. This chapter contained only a brief overview of arrays and their uses. Arrays will be described more fully in the programming projects to come.

Chapter 15

Pointers

A variable is really a location in the computer's memory. This location is known as its address. Every variable has an address. C allows you to access variables by using their addresses rather than their names. This is done with a special type of variable called a *pointer*. Instead of storing a value, a pointer stores the address of a variable.

Declaring a Pointer

When you declare a pointer, you must decide what kind of variable the pointer will point to. A pointer may hold the address of any variable type. The syntax for a pointer is

type *name;

Except for the asterisk, this is identical to a normal variable declaration. The asterisk tells C that the variable *name* holds the address of another variable of type *type*.

Using a Pointer

Figure 15-1 contains a simple program that will help illustrate how pointers are used.

Figure 15-1. Program Using Pointers

```
#include <stdio.h>

main()
{
        int a,b;              /* two integers */
        int *int_ptr;   /* A pointer to integers */

        a = 10;
        b = 5;

        int_ptr = &a;   /* 'int_ptr' holds the ADDRESS of 'a' */

        printf("'a' is %d, 'b' is %d, int_ptr points to %d\n",a,b,*int_ptr);
        a = 42;
        printf("'a' is %d, 'b' is %d, int_ptr points to %d\n",a,b,*int_ptr);
        *int_ptr = 56;
        printf("'a' is %d, 'b' is %d, int_ptr points to %d\n",a,b,*int_ptr);
        int_ptr = &b;
    printf("'a' is %d, 'b' is %d, int_ptr points to  %d\n",a,b,*int_ptr);
}
```

This program may confuse you. A couple of notes on syntax may help:

- The string *&a* means *the address of variable a.*
- The statement *int_ptr = &a* tells the computer to store the address of variable *a* in the pointer variable *int_ptr*. Note that *a* must be an integer if its address is to be stored in *int_ptr*.

The string **int_ptr* means *the variable int_ptr is pointing to.* When you use **int_ptr* in printf( ), C prints the value of the variable int_ptr is pointing to. When you assign a value to **int_ptr*, C stores the value in the variable *int_ptr* is pointing to.

Run this program (see Figure 15-2).

Figure 15-2. Results of Running the Program

```
'a' is 10, 'b' is 5, int_ptr points to  10
'a' is 42, 'b' is 5, int_ptr points to 42
'a' is 56, 'b' is 5, int_ptr points to 56
'a' is 56, 'b' is 5, int_ptr points to 5
```

```
Press any key to return to Turbo C . . .
```

Pointers can be a difficult concept to grasp. The key to understanding the previous program is to realize that there are only two integer variables being printed in each of the printf( ) statements.

The first thing this program does is create two integer variables and store the numbers 10 and 5 in them. See Figure 15-3.

Figure 15-3. Diagram of Two Declared Variables *a* and *b*

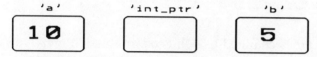

The variable *int_ptr* is then given the address of variable *a*. The variable *int_ptr* now points to variable *a* (Figure 15-4).

Figure 15-4. Address Pointer Variable *int_ptr* Points to Variable *a*

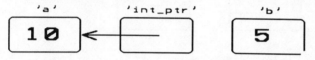

All of the printf( ) statements print three things:

• The value of *a*
• The value of *b*
• The value that *int_ptr* points to

In this case, *int_ptr* points to *a*, so you see *10 5 10* on the screen.

Next, the value of *a* is changed to 42. Because *int_ptr* still points to *a*, you'll see *42 5 42* on the screen. It seems as if you've changed two different variables, but you haven't; only *a* has been changed. (See Figure 15-5.)

Figure 15-5. Pointer *int_ptr* Still Points to Variable *a*

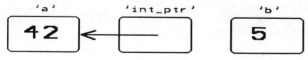

Next comes the instruction to change to 56 the variable *int_ptr* is pointing to. Since *int_ptr* is pointing to *a*, this is the same as changing *a*; thus, you see *56 5 56* on the screen (Figure 15-6).

Figure 15-6. Variable *a* Pointed to by *int_ptr* Changed to 56

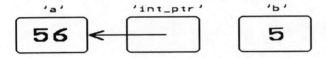

Finally, *int_ptr* is changed to point to variable *b*. Previously, **int_ptr* pointed to *a*. Now it points to *b*; thus, you see *56 5 5* on the screen (Figure 15-7).

Figure 15-7. Pointer Changed to Point to Variable *b*

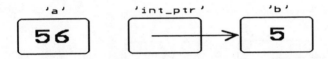

Arrays and Pointers

An array is actually a pointer. When you declare a normal variable, space for that single variable is created (Figure 15-8).

Figure 15-8. Space Reserved for Declared Variable

When you declare an array, space for all elements is created. A pointer is created and given the address of the first element. The addresses of the elements are sequential. If the address of the first element is 1523, the next will have an address of 1524, the next will be 1525, and so on. When you use an array with a statement like

```
array_name[element_number]
```

the *element_number* is added to the pointer *array_name* to find the address of the variable in question.

Consider Figure 15-9. This is an array of ten characters. When the array was declared, ten character variables were created with the addresses 1523–1533.

Figure 15-9. Ten-Element Array in Memory

'array_name'

```
1523 ┌─────────────┐
1524 │·············│
1525 │·············│
1526 │·············│
1527 │·············│
1528 │·············│
1529 │·············│
1530 │·············│
1531 │·············│
1532 └─────────────┘
```

At the same time, the pointer *array_name* is created, and the address 1523 is stored in it. Suppose you access an element in this array with a statement like

x = array_name[4];

The number 4 is added to the address in *array_name* (1523) to get the address of the fifth character (1527). (See Figure 15-10.)

Figure 15-10. Accessing Element 4 of Array *array_name*

'array_name'

```
1523 ┌─────────────┐ 0
1524 │·············│ 1
1525 │·············│ 2
1526 │·············│ 3
1527 │     5       │ 4
1528 │·············│ 5
1529 │·············│ 6
1530 │·············│ 7
1531 │·············│ 8
1532 └─────────────┘ 9
```

Figure 15-11 contains a program that will show you how an array might be used with pointers.

Figure 15-11. Demonstration Program Using Pointers

```
#include <stdio.h>

main()
{
        int i;
        float results[10];

        printf("Please enter 10 real numbers\n");

        for(i=0;i<10;i++)
        {
                printf("Number %d:",i+1);
                scanf("%f",results+i);
        }

        printf("The numbers have now been entered\n");
        printf("Enter a number between 1 and 10 to see\n");
        printf("a result, 0 to quit\n");

        do
        {
                printf(":");
                scanf("%d",&i);
                if(i > 0 && i < 11)      /* a legal element (1-10) */
        printf("Element %d contains %f\n",i,*(results+i-1));
                                /* Elements range from 0 to 9 */
        }
        while(i != 0);
}
```

This is the array example from the last chapter except that all array references have been changed to pointer references. The first change in this program is the line

scanf("%f",results+i);

How does this work? Remember that an array is really a pointer to the first variable in a sequential list of variables. These variables are all the same size. Any addition to the array pointer is automatically multiplied by the size of the data type in the array, giving the address of that element of the array. For instance, results+0 is the same as results[0], results+1 is the same as results[1], and so on.

Another thing you may have noticed is that there is no & in front of results. In past examples, variables passed to scanf( ) were always preceded by an &. This is because the parameters to the scanf( ) function are really pointers. The ampersand operator signals the compiler to create a pointer to the variable by passing its address. Since results is already a pointer, there is no need for the &.

The second change in this program is in the final printf statement. Instead of results[i-1], we now have *(results+i-1). Since the user will enter numbers 1–10, and the array ranges from 0 to 9, 1 must be subtracted from the index to get the correct element. The * operator then returns the value that this pointer points to.

Dynamic Arrays

When you write a program using an array, you must know exactly how big that array is going to be before you compile the program. This can cause difficulties if you don't know exactly how much information needs to be stored in the array. Suppose you wanted to keep a list of telephone numbers. How can you know in advance how many telephone numbers you'll need? You could leave a large area free, potentially wasting memory that might be better used in another way. Or you could make your best guess as to your storage needs and worry about whether you've left enough space each time you add a new number. Wouldn't it be nice if C were flexible enough to expand the array to whatever size was needed? Well, it is. The structure that allows you to specify the size of the array at runtime is called a dynamic array.

The next example will show you a program that is a modification of the original array program. Figure 15-12 represents a new version of the program in Figure 14-5. When it is compiled and run, it will ask how many numbers you want to store and then will create an array of exactly that size.

Figure 15-12. A Program Using Dynamic Arrays

```
#include <stdio.h>
main()
{
        int i,elements;
        float *results;

        printf("How many numbers ? ");
        scanf("%d",&elements);

        results = (float *)malloc(elements * sizeof(float));

        printf("Please enter %d real numbers\n",elements);

        for(i=0;i<elements;i++)
        {
                printf("Number %d:",i+1);
                scanf("%f",&results[i]);
        }

        printf("The numbers have now been entered\n");
        printf("Enter a number between 1 and %d to see\n",elements);
        printf("a result, 0 to quit\n");

        do
        {
                printf(":");
                scanf("%d",&i);
                if(i > 0 && i < elements+1)
                    printf("Element %d contains %f\n",i,results[i-1]);
        }
        while(i != 0);
}
```

This is done using the function malloc( ) and the sizeof operator. The sizeof operater returns the size (in bytes) of an object. Malloc( ) takes a single integer as a parameter and creates an array able to hold that number of characters. It will then return a pointer to this array. For example, the following statement would create enough space for 12 characters, six integers, or three floating-point variables.

```
malloc(12);
```

You can then assign this value to a pointer of the appropriate type. When you do this, you must tell C what type of array malloc( ) is to create. You could create an array of integers. In this case malloc( ) should return a pointer to an integer ((int *)malloc). You could be creating an array of characters, in which case malloc( ) should return a character pointer. In order to tell C which type to use, place the type in parentheses before malloc( ). This is called type casting. To create an array of 12 characters, use the following:

```
char *a;
a = (char *) malloc(12);
```

Type casting can actually be used on any value or function. A type cast converts the value following it into the type specified. For example,

```
(int) 4.5
```

would convert the value 4.5 into the integer 4. Malloc( ) needs to know what type of pointer to return. In the above example, you told malloc( ) to return a character pointer.

Using malloc( ), you can create a pointer that points to a set of variables in the same way an array does. In the previous example, you were shown that you could treat an array just like a pointer. The converse is also true. You can create a pointer and treat it just like an array.

Convert the old version of the program so that it asks the user for a number. Then, instead of using an array, use malloc( ) to create an array big enough to hold this number of floats (Figure 15-12).

Note that sizeof( ) is used in the malloc( ) statement to determine the proper size of the array. You know that the number of elements is in the variable *elements*. In order to determine the size of the entire array, this must be multiplied by the size of each individual element.

Compare the two versions of this program in Figures 14-5 and 15-12. If you understand these changes, then you understand how pointers can be used to create a dynamic array. As mentioned above, a dynamic array is simply an array whose size is not known until the program is run.

Strings as Dynamic Arrays

As you saw in the previous chapter, strings are a type of array. Using standard arrays, strings can be difficult to manipulate. When you need to put a string into a character array, you must use the standard function strcpy( ).

If you use dynamic character arrays, the strcpy( ) is not necessary.

When a pointer is created to point to an array, C puts certain restrictions on it. Such a pointer may never be changed; it must always point to the original array.

When C sees the expression "This is a string", it creates a new character array and places the letters *This is a string* in it. This array is not given a name, however. Instead, such an expression returns an address that points to the beginning of the string.

The strcpy( ) function takes addresses as parameters. This explains how the statement *strcpy(str,"This is a string")* works. Both parameters are addresses of character arrays. The contents of the string at the second address are copied to the first address.

If the destination string is not an array, there is an easier way of doing this. Consider the following declaration:

char *str = "This is a string";

The first part of this statement creates a pointer to a char with the name *str*. The address of *"This is a string"* is then placed in the pointer *str*, which can then be used like any normal string. Figure 15-13 shows how this could be used in a program.

Figure 15-13. Program Using Dynamic Strings

```
#include <stdio.h>

main()
{
     char * str = "This is the first string\n";

     printf(str);
     str = "This is the second string\n";
     printf(str);
     str = "This is the last string\n";
     printf(str);
}
```

Now suppose str was declared to be an array of chars (see Figure 15-14).

Figure 15-14. Declaring a Character Array

```
#include <stdio.h>

main()
{
     char str[80] = "This is the first string\n";

     printf(str);
     str = "This is the second string\n";
     printf(str);
     str = "This is the last string\n";
     printf(str);
}
```

Try compiling this program. When it is run, you're given many error messages. When you try to assign a string to a character array, you're attempting to change the value of the pointer that points to the array, which is illegal in C.

Summary
In this chapter, you've learned how to declare and use a pointer. You've also seen how pointers can be used to replace the relatively rigid array structure with a dynamic array. You've learned how to incorporate the malloc( ) and sizeof( )

functions into your programs to work with dynamic arrays. Finally, you've learned a new way of dealing with strings as dynamic arrays.

Pointers and string manipulation are difficult subjects. You've only seen the basics in this chapter. It's very difficult to learn how these things work without actually seeing an example of a large-scale program. The last section of this book will show you three such programs. In these chapters, you'll learn the details of how pointers work.

Chapter 16
Structure Variables

Earlier you learned how to tie a number of variables (of a single type) together under a single name as an array. In this chapter, you'll learn how to tie a number of variables with different types together under a single name. In C, such a variable grouping is called a structure.

Structures

A structure is not identical to an array. Whereas the elements of an array don't have names of their own, members of a structure do. A structure merely provides a way for the programmer to tie related variables to one another.

The syntax for a structure is

```
struct name
{
Declaration list;
} variable_list;
```

Name is an optional name you wish to give to the structure type. The declaration list is simply a list of variable declarations. These variables will be bound together under the structure name. *Variable_list* is a list of the variables you wish to have in this structure. Here is a simple structure declaration:

```
struct
{
    char name[50];
    char address[50];
    char phone[14];
    int zip, id;
}person;
```

This creates one structure type without giving it a name. It creates one variable of this type and calls it *person. Person* contains five variables:

- Three strings
  - *name*
  - *address*
  - *phone*
- Two ints
  - *zip*
  - *id*

Each of these variables may be used independently or, as you'll see later, the entire structure may be accessed as a single entity.

To access a member of a structure, use the following syntax:

```
structure_name.variable_name
```

For example, to assign the contents of the variable *my_zip* to the variable *zip* in the structure *person,* you'd use the statement:

```
person.zip = my_zip;
```

Person.zip can be used just like a normal int variable. For all intents and purposes, *person.zip* is a normal integer.

Why have structures at all? It just seems like a more difficult way of naming variables. Why not use the following declaration instead?

```
char person_name[50];
char person_address[50];
char person_phone[15];
int person_id,person_zip;
```

The real power behind structures becomes apparent when they're used with the typedef command. The next section will describe the uses of this command.

Typedef

The typedef command allows you to create new variable types. These new types then can be used to declare variables just like any of the basic types (int, char, or float). To use typedef, simply place it before any legal variable declaration. That variable declaration then becomes a type declaration. The following example creates a new variable type called money whose structure is the same as the float type.

```
typedef float money;
```

This may then be used to create new variables:

```
money my_cash, his_cash;
```

The new variable type money can then be used to declare variables in the same way as the old variable type float.

Typedef statements are nearly always made global so that the type is available throughout the program. This is not required, however. A type may be either global or local just like a variable. A local type declaration may only be used to declare variables in the block in which it is created. A global type declaration may be used to declare variables anywhere in that file.

This is not very exciting in itself. Why rename a type? Nothing new is gained. Typedef is not restricted to simple types, however. Suppose you wanted to create a string type. You could use typedef with an array declaration as in Figure 16-1.

Figure 16-1. Creating a String Variable Type

```
#include <stdio.h>

typedef char string[80];

main()
{
        string a,b;

        strcpy(a,"This is a test");
        strcpy(b,"of typedef");

        printf("the string is '%s %s'\n",a,b);

}
```

The real power of typedef resides in the fact that you may use any simple type as a parameter. String is now a simple variable type, so it may be used as a parameter. Figure 16-2 contains a procedure that takes two arguments of type string and prints them.

Figure 16-2. Using String Type Variables as Parameters

```
print_em(a,b)
string a,b;
{
        printf("The string is '%s %s'\n",a,b);
}
```

You must be careful with typedef. In the function in Figure 16-3, you might be tempted to assign one string to another. Keep in mind that these are still arrays of characters even though the type name has been changed.

Figure 16-3. Program Illegally Assigns One String Type Variable to Another

```
#include <stdio.h>

typedef char string[80];

main()
{
        string a,b;

        strcpy(b,"This is a test");
        b = a;

        printf("the string is '%s %s'\n",a,b);

}
```

If you try running the program Figure 16-3, you'll encounter an error. The variable *a* could not be assigned to the variable *b* because they're both arrays. Even though the type was renamed, you still couldn't assign one array to another.

Typedef and Structures

Typedef is usually used with structures. In Figure 16-4, instead of declaring a single structure called *person*, a new variable type with this name is declared.

Figure 16-4. A New Variable Type Replaces Structure

```
#include <stdio.h>

typedef struct person {
        char name[80];
        char street[80];
        int ID;
} person;

read_info(a_person)
struct person *a_person;
{
        printf("Enter the person's name: ");
        scanf("%s", a_person->name);
        printf("Enter the street that %s lives on: ", a_person->name);
        scanf("%s", a_person->street);
        printf("Enter %s's ID number: ", a_person->name );
        scanf("%d", &(a_person->ID) );
}


main()
{

        person people[5]; /* The array people has 5 elements. Each
                             element is a person structure */
        int i;

        for ( i = 0;  i < 5;  i++ )
        {
                printf("Enter information for person %d\n", i+1);
                read_info(&people[i]);
        }
        printf("The name of person 2 is %s\n", people[1].name);
}
```

After this declaration, you can use the new type person to declare new variables. Because each of these variables is of a single type, they can be used interchangeably.

In main( ), you create an array of five elements. Each element is a structure of type person. Each element has all the variables of a person structure, including *name, street,* and *id.* In the *for* loop, a pointer to each successive element is passed to the function read_info( ). This function can then access each of the individual elements of *person* as if they were normal pointer variables. The program is greatly simplified because you're able to treat each *person* as a single object rather than as a group of variables. Imagine the difficulties of manipulating the data in Figure 16-6 if structures were not allowed. You'd have to create five separate arrays for each of the variables in *person.*

Here you were introduced to the -> operator. This is known as the *structure pointer operator.* As mentioned above, a pointer is passed to each individual structure in the *people* array. If you're passing a pointer to a structure, how can you access individual variables within the structure? At first, you

might think that you could use *a_person.name* to access the
variable *name* in the structure *a_person* is pointing to. Unfortunately, the . operator has a higher precedence than the * operator. Instead of accessing the variable *name* within the
structure that *a_person* is pointing to, this would attempt to
access the variable *name* from a structure and use it as a
pointer. This clearly isn't what you want. One solution would
be to use parentheses to perform the pointer indirection first,
as in *(*a_person).name*. That means "go to the structure
a_person is pointing to and refer to the variable *name* in that
structure." This type of operation is done so frequently that a
new operator was created to do exactly the same thing.

(*a_person).name

can be written as

a_person->name

This is a shorthand method of accessing a variable within
a structure through the use of a pointer.

Summary
This chapter described structures only very briefly. You
haven't yet seen the full power of structures, nor have you
seen all the ways structures may be used. The next chapter
will use a simple database program to help explain how structures, as well as arrays and pointers, can be used in a real
program.

Section Five
Programs

Chapter 17
The Database

The examples presented in the previous chapters served only to show how the different parts of the C language fit together. The next three chapters will show how C can be used to write programs you'll find useful.

Database programs can be very complicated, filling hundreds of pages of code. They can also be extremely simple. Large or small, all databases share some basic features. This chapter will show you how structures and arrays can be used to create a simple database.

A database is a tool for storing and retrieving information. In their highest form, database programs can store almost any information, allowing near-instant retrieval of any data in the system. The program in this chapter will be far simpler. It will only be able to store names and addresses and a limited amount of data. It will be sufficiently complex, however, to show you the structure of most database programs.

Most database programs are centered around a single data structure. This data structure is used to store all information. A small number of routines then are written to operate on that data structure. This chapter will describe three of the four most common operations. The first, insert( ), places information into the data structure. The second, get( ), retrieves information from the data structure. A third less-important operation is print( ), which will print the entire contents of the database. Most databases will also include a delete( ) function, which will remove information from the database. With the information gained in this chapter, you should have little trouble implementing delete( ) yourself.

Parts of a Database

The database is composed of individual parts. The most important are the record and the field.

Records. The basic unit of information in a database is the record. A record is a set of related pieces of data. In this programming example, the record is composed of the name, address, and phone number of a single person. Given one piece of information in a record, a database program will be able to find the other information in that record.

Fields. Each separate piece of information in a record is called a field. In C, a structure is ideal for storing a record. A structure is able to tie together a number of different variables under a single name. Each variable represents one field.

Key fields. In a database, all records will share one or more key fields. A key field is simply a field that is used to find the values of other fields. In this example, the user will usually have the name of the person and will wish to find the address and phone number associated with it. The name is the key field. The program could be written to find a person's name based on the phone number. In that case, the phone number would be considered the key field.

Values in the key field should be unique. No two people should have the same name. This rule is not a requirement of databases, but it does make them easier to construct.

Designing a Database

The first task in designing a database is to create the basic record structure. This can be done in a simple typedef instruction. You need to create a single structure that contains a set of strings containing a name, street address, city, state, zip code, and phone number for a single person as shown in Figure 17-1.

Figure 17-1. Defining the Structure to Serve as the Record

```
typedef struct record_name
{
     char name[21];
     char address[41];
     char city[20];
     char st[3];
     char zip[6];
     char phone[13];
}record;
```

Now you need to tie these records together in a single data structure. There are many ways of doing this. This chapter will present one of the simplest. An array is useful for tying together large numbers of identical variables. In this case, each element of the array would be a structure of type person (Figure 17-2).

Figure 17-2. An Array of Structures

The Database

Name
Address
Phone
Name
Address
Phone
Name
Address
Phone
Name
Address
Phone

Using an array of structures can be inefficient, however. If you have an array of 1000 structures of type person, you'll use almost 100K of memory. Such an array will contain 1000 structures regardless of whether or not all the structures have information in them.

Ideally, you don't want to use memory unless you have information to put in it. There are a number of ways to do this. Most are very complex and are beyond the scope of this book.

There is one fairly simple data structure that will help you cut down tremendously on the amount of memory used. Instead of putting structures in an array, put pointers to those structures in the array. When a record is created, malloc( ) will be used to reserve the memory for the record. One of the pointers then will be used to point to the block of memory (Figure 17-3).

Figure 17-3. An Array of Pointers Saves Memory

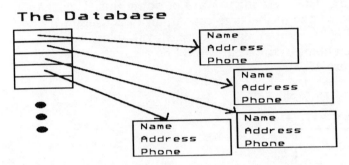

The structure shown in Figure 17-1 occupies approximately 100 bytes. If you have 1000 of these structures, 100K will be occupied. One thousand pointers to these records will only occupy 1000 × 4 bytes, or about 4K. You still need 100 bytes per record but only for records that are actually used.

An array of pointers can be declared easily as in Figure 17-4.

Figure 17-4. Declaring list_of_records As an Array of Pointers

```
record *list_of_records[number_of_records];
int record_ptr = 0;
```

Here, *list_of_records* is declared as an array of pointers to structures. If there are 1000 pointers to structures and only 100 structures, some of these pointers will be undefined. You need to keep track of which pointers point to valid structures. With an array, this can be done with a single integer. This is the purpose of the variable *record_ptr* in Figure 17-4. This variable stores the number of structures currently in use. It is 0 when the program begins.

Insertion

Now that the data structure has been created, you need a function to place data in it. This function will take a structure of type person and will place a pointer to it in the proper place in the array. Where is the proper place? To make things slightly more interesting, the function in Figure 17-5 will keep the list in sorted order.

Figure 17-5. Function to Keep List in Sorted Order

```
void insert(record *a)
{
    int i=0, temp_ptr=1;
    record *new_record;

    new_record = (record *)malloc(sizeof(record));
    strcpy( new_record->name, a->name );
    strcpy( new_record->address, a->address );
    strcpy( new_record->city, a->city );
    strcpy( new_record->st, a->st );
    strcpy( new_record->zip, a->zip );
    strcpy( new_record->phone, a->phone );
    record_ptr++;
    if ( record_ptr > 1 )
    {
        while (strcmp(list_of_records[temp_ptr]->name,new_record->name)<0 &&
                temp_ptr < record_ptr )
            temp_ptr++;
        for ( i = record_ptr;  i > temp_ptr;  i-- )
            list_of_records[i] = list_of_records[i-1];
    }
    else
        temp_ptr = 1;
    list_of_records[temp_ptr] = new_record;
}
```

This function first creates a new record and copies the data to it. It then adds 1 to the total number of records. If this total equals 1, the insertion task is easy: This is the first record, just place it at the beginning of the list. Otherwise, the program must determine where in the list this record should go.

A new variable called *temp_ptr* then is used to search through the list of structures. A *while* loop is used to compare the names in each of the structures to the name in the record being inserted. Consider the following statement:

    while(stricmp(list_of_records[temp_ptr]->name,new_record->name)<0

In the *while* loop, you compare two names (two strings) with stricmp( ). This standard C function takes two character strings as parameters. If the first string is alphabetically first, it will return a negative number. If the second string is alphabetically first, it will return a positive number. If the two strings are equal, it will return 0.

This *while* loop goes through the list of structures one by one until it finds a record whose name does not come before the name of the record to be inserted (see Figure 17-6).

Figure 17-6. Searching for Slot for Pointer Insertion

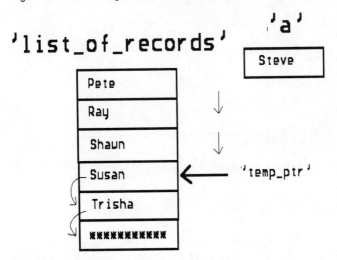

'list_of_records'   'a'

The second condition in the loop, *temp_ptr < record_ptr*, ensures that the program will only search existing structures.

After this loop ends, the variable *temp_ptr* will contain the location in the array in which the new record will be placed. This index may already contain a record, however. If this is so, all structures above the insertion point must be moved to make way for the new record. This is done in the *for* loop. Starting at the top of the array, each record pointer is moved up exactly one index. This continues down the array until the insertion point is reached. The new record can now be inserted here.

If there are no structures in the array, *temp_ptr* is set to 1: There is no need to find the correct insertion point. In this case, the insertion point will always be the first location in the array.

The function insert( ) is the most complicated part of this program. As you'll see, once a record has been inserted correctly, the rest of the program becomes relatively simple.

Retrieving Data

Once data has been inserted into the database, you'd like to be able to look at it. The function get( ) will do this. This function will take a single record and will search for a record in the database that contains the same name. If a match is found, a pointer to the matching record is returned to the main program, otherwise −1 is returned to indicate an error.

The array is searched using a simple *for* loop. The *name* field of each record in the array is compared to the *name* field in the parameter *a* with stricmp( ). As you'll recall, this will return 0 if the two strings are the same. The single exclamation point is the *not* operator. This operator takes any logical value and returns its opposite. Thus, *!FALSE* is true and *!TRUE* is false. You'll recall that 0 is false. The stricmp( ) function will return false (0) if the two strings are equal, so !stricmp( ) will return true if the strings are equal.

If the conditional statement finds a record in the array whose name matches the name passed in the parameter *a*, the record is sent back to the main program with a return statement. This causes execution of the function to end immediately. What if no match was found? Returning a −1 is a fairly standard way to indicate an error, but this function expects to return a pointer to a *person*. The solution is to use the type casting. The statement return(record *) −1 will convert the −1 to the proper form and pass it back to the main program.

The next two functions concern file access and will be discussed later. They allow you to store data on your disk. Without these functions, you'd have to reenter all the data every time you run the program.

Printing

The final function is print( ) (Figure 17-7).

Figure 17-7. The print( ) Function

```
void print()
{
    int i;

    if ( record_ptr > 0 )
        for ( i = 1;  i <= record_ptr;  i++ )
            cprintf("%d:%s %s\n", i, list_of_records[i]->name,\
                    list_of_records[i]->city );
    else
        cprintf("No records\n");
}
```

209

This function will print the contents of the array to the screen. As you can see, it is not a very complicated function. If there are structures in the array, the function prints one by one the *name* and *city* fields found in them. If there are no structures, then the message *No records* is printed to the screen. The only confusing part about this function is cprintf( ). You haven't previously seen this function. It is identical to printf( ) in most respects and allows you take advantage of some special viewport functions found in *Turbo C 1.5*.

Viewports. A viewport is simply a section of the screen used for printing. Cprintf( ) will never print anything outside the bounds of the viewport. The viewport becomes a little screen. Nothing outside of the viewport will ever be affected by cprintf( ).

The function main( ) uses the database functions just presented. In this program, four viewports are defined (Figure 17-8).

Figure 17-8. Four Viewports Defined

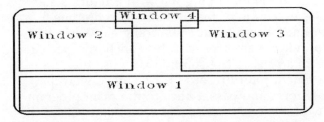

Four sections of the screen are used to present four types of information. The first section will contain the list of options available from the program. The second will be used to ask for data from the user. The third will be used by print( ) to show the contents of the array. The last section will be used to send messages to the user.

Windows are created with the function window( ). Window( ) takes four integer parameters. These designate the size of the window. The first parameter gives the column number (1–80) of the left side of the window. The second parameter gives the row number (1–25) of the top of the window. The third parameter defines the column number of the right edge of the window. The fourth parameter defines the row number of the bottom edge of the window. When any C program begins, a single window is automatically created to fill the entire screen:

window(1,1,80,25)

In the database program, four macros have been defined to simplify the task of switching between windows. Each of these macro functions contains two statements. The first statement in each defines the window. The second defines the color which cprintf( ) will use to print. To print to a window, you simply use the appropriate macro and use cprintf( ) as you would printf( ).

The Main Program

Figure 17-9 contains a listing of the entire program.

Figure 17-9. Database Program

```c
#include <stdio.h>
#include <string.h>
#include <alloc.h>
#include <graphics.h>
#include <fcntl.h>
#include <sys\stat.h>

#define WINDOW1() window(1,16,80,25); textcolor(CYAN);
#define WINDOW2() window(1,5,40,12); textcolor(GREEN);
#define WINDOW3() window(41,5,80,12); textcolor(RED);
#define WINDOW4() window(20,3,40,4); textcolor(MAGENTA);
#define number_of_records 500

typedef struct record_name
{
        char name[21];
        char address[41];
        char city[20];
        char st[3];
        char zip[6];
        char phone[13];
} record;

record *list_of_records[number_of_records];
int record_ptr=0;

void insert(record *);
record *get(record *);
void print(void);
void save(void);
void load(void);

void insert(record *a)
{
   int i=0, temp_ptr=1;
   record *new_record;

   new_record = (record *)malloc(sizeof(record));
   strcpy( new_record->name, a->name );
   strcpy( new_record->address, a->address );
   strcpy( new_record->city, a->city );
   strcpy( new_record->st, a->st );
   strcpy( new_record->zip, a->zip );
   strcpy( new_record->phone, a->phone );
   record_ptr++;
   if ( record_ptr > 1 )
   {
```

```
        while ( strcmp(list_of_records[temp_ptr]->name, new_record->name) < 0 &&
                temp_ptr < record_ptr )
            temp_ptr++;
        for ( i = record_ptr;  i > temp_ptr;  i-- )
            list_of_records[i] = list_of_records[i-1];
    )
    else
        temp_ptr = 1;
    list_of_records[temp_ptr] = new_record;
)


record *get(record *a)
(
    int i;

    for ( i = 1;  i <= record_ptr;  i++ )
        if ( !stricmp(list_of_records[i]->name, a->name ))

            return( list_of_records[i] );
    return(record *) -1;
)

void save()
(
    int i, file;

    file = open("base.dat", O_CREAT | O_RDWR | O_TEXT, S_IREAD | S_IWRITE );
    write( file, &record_ptr, sizeof(int) );
    for ( i = 1;  i <= record_ptr;  i++ )
        write( file, list_of_records[i], sizeof(record) );
    close( file );
)

void load()
(
    int i, file;

    file = open("base.dat", O_RDWR | O_TEXT );
    read( file, &record_ptr, sizeof(int) );
    for ( i = 1;  i <= record_ptr;  i++ )
    (
        list_of_records[i] = (record *)malloc(sizeof(record));
        read( file, list_of_records[i], sizeof(record) );
    )
    close( file );
)


void print()
(
    int i;

    if ( record_ptr > 0 )
        for ( i = 1;  i <= record_ptr;  i++ )
            cprintf("%d:%s %s\n", i, list_of_records[i]->name,\
                    list_of_records[i]->city );
    else
        cprintf("No records\n");
)


main()
(
    char ch;
    record person;
    record *rec;

    clrscr();
    WINDOW1();
    clrscr();
    cprintf("I)nsert\nG)et\nE)dit\nP)rint all\nS)ave\nL)oad\nQ)uit");
    do
    (
        WINDOW1();
        ch = getch();
        switch( ch )
        (
            case 'I' :
            case 'i' :
```

```
                    WINDOW2();
                    clrscr();
                    cprintf("Name: ");
                    gets( person.name );
                    cprintf("Address: ");
        gets( person.address );
        cprintf("City: ");
        gets( person.city );
        cprintf("St: ");
        gets( person.st );
        cprintf("Zip: ");
        gets( person.zip );
        cprintf("Phone: ");
        gets( person.phone );
        insert( &person );
        break;
case 'G' :
case 'g' :
    WINDOW2();
    clrscr();
    cprintf("Name: ");
    gets( person.name );
    rec = get( &person );
    if ( rec != (record *) -1 )
    {
        WINDOW3();
        clrscr();
        cprintf("\n%s\n", rec->name );
        cprintf("%s\n", rec->address );
        cprintf("%s", rec->city );
        cprintf(", %s", rec->st );
        cprintf("   %s\n", rec->zip );
        cprintf("%s", rec->phone );
    }
    else
        cprintf("Not found!\n");
    break;
case 'E' :
case 'e' :
    WINDOW2();
    clrscr();
    cprintf("Name: ");
    gets( person.name );
    rec = get( &person );
    if ( rec != (record *) -1 )
    {
        WINDOW3();
        clrscr();
        cprintf("\n%s\n", rec->name );
        cprintf("%s\n", rec->address );
        cprintf("%s", rec->city );
        cprintf(", %s", rec->st );
        cprintf("   %s\n", rec->zip );
        cprintf("%s", rec->phone );
        WINDOW2();
        clrscr();
        cprintf("Name: ");
        gets( rec->name );
        cprintf("Address: ");
        gets( rec->address );
        cprintf("City: ");
        gets( rec->city );
        cprintf("St: ");
        gets( rec->st );
        cprintf("Zip: ");
        gets( rec->zip );
        cprintf("Phone: ");
        gets( rec->phone );
    }
    else
        cprintf("Not found!\n");
                    break;
            case 'P' :
            case 'p' :
                WINDOW3();
                clrscr();
                print();
                break;
            case 'S' :
            case 's' :
```

```
         WINDOW4();
         clrscr();
         cprintf("Saving...\n");
         save();
         clrscr();
         break;
    case 'L' :
    case 'l' :
         WINDOW4();
         clrscr();
         cprintf("Loading...\n");
         load();
         clrscr();
         break;
    case 'Q' :
    case 'q' :
         break;
    default : putchar(7);
              break;
   }
 }
 while( ch != 'q' );
}
```

Consider main( ). First, the function clrscr( ) is used to clear the screen. Then, the macro WINDOW1( ) is used to switch to the first window. A menu is then printed in this window. The rest of main( ) consists of a large switch statement inside a *do* loop.

At the beginning of this loop, a character is read from the keyboard with getch( ). The switch statement will then execute a certain section of code depending on the option chosen.

The first option is the insert option. If the user presses the I key (upper- or lowercase), the code controlled by the first case statement will execute. This section of code will switch to the second window and erase its contents with clrscr( ). (Note that this only affects the second window. The menu in window 1 is not erased.) Next, the user is prompted to enter information in each of the fields of the *person* record.

A new function, gets( ), is used to read each character string. If you'll recall, strings read by scanf( ) are separated by spaces. This will not read a name correctly as most names will have spaces in them. Gets( ) will read a string with spaces in it. It takes one parameter—the string to read. Everything up to the end of the line will be placed in that string.

Notice the syntax of the structure access. In main, *person* is declared as *record person*, not *record *person*. Because it is not a pointer, the period rather than the arrow (->) must be used to access each field in the structure.

Finally, the structure *person* is sent to insert( ). Insert( ) expects a pointer to a structure. You can send it a pointer by using the ampersand (&) to send the address of the structure *person* to insert( ). Once the record is inserted, a break statement is used to exit the switch statement.

If the user chooses the get option, the second section of code is executed. This code also switches to the second window and clears the screen. The user is then prompted for a name. This name is then placed in the record *person* which is then sent to the function get( ). Get( ) returns a record which is then assigned to another record pointer, *rec*.

If get( ) returns a value of −1, then the record was not found. If a record was found, the contents of that record then are printed to window 3 with cprintf( ). Pointer *rec* is not a structure, but a pointer to a structure, so the structure pointer operator must be used to access each field.

The next option is the edit option. It allows the user to change data already in the database. First, the user is prompted to enter a name. This name is stored in the variable *rec*. Next, the function get( ) is used to search for a database record that contains this name. If a match is not found, the message *Not found!* is printed. If a match is found, the values in this record are printed to window 3. New values for this record are then read from window 2. Because *rec* points to a record in the database, any changes made to *rec* will automatically change the record in the database.

The next three options allow you to print the contents of the database to the screen, save the database to disk, and read the database from disk. In each case, a window is cleared and the corresponding function called. Print( ) was described above, the other two functions will be described later in this chapter.

Quit is the option used to exit the program.

The last case is unusual. Most switch statements have a special case called default. This case is automatically chosen if no other case matches the switch variable. In this switch statement, the default action is to send character number 7 to the screen with the function putchar( ). Character 7 is a special character that causes the computer to beep when it is printed. The program uses this character to make the computer beep when a letter not corresponding to a command is entered.

File Handling

The routines save( ) and load( ) were saved for last because they really aren't part of the database itself. Instead, they allow you to save the database to disk and then later read it back in.
   There are three steps to using a file.

• You must first open the file with open( ). This allows the program to access the file with a file handle. A file handle is simply a number used by DOS to refer to a file.
• Once the file is opened, data can be accessed with read( ) and write( ).
• When the program is through with the file, the file must be closed with close( ).

   Opening a file. Open( ) takes three parameters:

• The filename
• The file descriptor
• The file access parameter

   A file descriptor is a set of flags describing the file. Consider the following open statement used in save( ):

```
open("base.dat",O_CREAT | O_RDWR | O_TEXT, S_IREAD |
    S_IWRITE);
```

   The first parameter tells open( ) to open the file *base.dat*. The second parameter is a set of three flags. O_CREAT tells open( ) to create the file if it does not already exist. O_RDWR tells open( ) to allow both reading and writing. O_TEXT tells open( ) that the file is a text file. These flags must be separated by the bitwise OR operator.
   The final parameter is a set of access flags. These are only used when the file is created. The first, S_IREAD, tells DOS that anyone may be allowed to read the file. The second, S_IWRITE, tells DOS that anyone may be allowed to write to the file.
   Saving a file. Look at save( ) in Figure 17-10.

Figure 17-10. The save( ) Function

```
void save()
{
    int i, file;

    file = open("base.dat", O_CREAT | O_RDWR | O_TEXT, S_IREAD | S_IWRITE );
    write( file, &record_ptr, sizeof(int) );
    for ( i = 1;  i <= record_ptr;  i++ )
        write( file, list_of_records[i], sizeof(record) );
    close( file );
}

void load()
{
    int i, file;

    file = open("base.dat", O_RDWR | O_TEXT );
    read( file, &record_ptr, sizeof(int) );
    for ( i = 1;  i <= record_ptr;  i++ )
    {
        list_of_records[i] = (record *)malloc(sizeof(record));
        read( file, list_of_records[i], sizeof(record) );
    }
    close( file );
}
```

The file is opened as described above, and the file handle is placed in the variable *file*. Now the contents of the database can be saved to the file named base.dat. This is done in two steps. First the contents of the variable *record_ptr* are stored to disk with write( ). Three parameters are taken by write( ):

• The file handle of the file to write to
• The variable to be written to the file
• The size of that variable

Once *record_ptr* is written, the contents of the array are written to the file with a *for* loop. Elements are sent to write( ) one by one. Note that write( ) must be given the size of each element to work properly. Sizeof( ) works as well with user-defined types as it does with the standard types so it can be used for this purpose.

After all data is written, the file must be closed. This can be done with a single close( ) statement. This function takes only a single parameter: the file handle of the file to be closed.

Loading a file. Load( ) works in a manner similar to save( ). First, the file is opened. Because the file already exists, the O_CREAT and access flags (S_IREAD and S_IWRITE) are not used. Next, the variable *record_ptr* is read from the file. The record_ptr variable will contain the number of records to

217

read from the file. Notice that the parameters used with read( ) are identical to the parameters used with write( ). You must give read( ) a file handle, a variable, and the size of that variable.

Once you have the length of the array from the file, you can use a simple *for* loop to read the structures into the array. Note that the order that variables are read from the disk is the same as the order in which they were written. You must always make sure your reads and writes match. The only way a program can determine which information belongs in each variable is by the order of the information in the file.

Header Files

The only thing in Figure 17-9 left undescribed is the list of header files at the beginning. You already know stdio.h. In order to use string manipulations, you must include string.h. It contains the header information for functions like stricmp( ). The header alloc.h contains the prototype for malloc( ). The headers fcntl.h and stat.h contain header material for the file-handling routines.

You'll find that this program can be useful for storing short lists of names and addresses. While this program is functional, it cannot compare to a large database. There are many enhancements that could be made that are left up to the reader. One of the most obvious is the delete( ) function. You presently have no way of deleting a record. This is a relatively simple task. First, you must find the record as you did in get( ). Next, use the function free( ) on the record pointer to tell C that you no longer need that memory space. Finally, move all pointers above the deleted record down one slot in the array.

Before going on, you may want to think about delete( ) some more and consider what other changes you could make. For example, how could this program keep more than one file? Is there a more efficient way to find a record than the linear search presented here? How would you print the list sorted by address rather than by name? These problems sound simple but can actually be quite difficult. Whole books have been written on database management alone.

Summary

The primary focus of this chapter was on creating a database written in C. While exploring that territory, many other areas were covered. You learned that a database is composed of records and files, which are roughly analogous to structures and arrays. You found out that storing an array of pointers rather than an array of structures can save memory. You should now know how to sort arrays and how to insert a pointer into its proper place within an array. You also learned how to retrieve information with getchar( ).

Windows were covered in a section on printing infor-mation to the screen. File access was also covered. Finally there was a brief explanation of the header files used in the database program.

Chapter 18
The Graphics Program

The previous chapter introduced you to some serious programming: database management. This chapter will ignore serious programming issues and will instead show you how to use the *Turbo C* graphics libraries to create interesting animated pictures. The recent release of *Turbo C* 1.5 introduced a complete library of graphics commands. These commands can be used to create fast and professional-looking graphics with little effort. This chapter will describe a program that uses some of these routines.

Graphics Mode
The IBM PC operates in two different modes. The first is called text mode. In text mode, only characters, such as letters, numbers, and various symbols can be sent to the screen. No other graphics of any type may be used. In graphics mode, anything at all may be drawn on the screen. You may draw shapes of many different kinds, and you may also write text using special *Turbo C* graphics library commands.

Using graphics in *Turbo C* is a four-step process:

- First, you must determine what kind of graphics hardware is available to the system. This is done using a *Turbo C* graphics command.
- Once your program determines what type of graphics hardware is available, it must pick the correct graphics mode. There are actually a great number of graphics modes available. Your choice will depend on the hardware available and the resolution and number of colors you need.
- Once it has determined the mode, your program will use another *Turbo C* command to initialize the graphics system in this mode. You may then use any of the *Turbo C* graphics commands.
- When you have finished using graphics, you'll use a final graphics command to return the screen to text mode.

Figure 18-1 contains a program that uses a number of graphics commands.

Figure 18-1. Program Using Graphics Commands

```
#include <graphics.h>
#include <stdio.h>
#include <conio.h>
#include <process.h>

int g_driver, g_mode, g_error;
int MAX_X,MAX_Y,MIN_X,MIN_Y;

start_graph()
{
        detectgraph(&g_driver, &g_mode);

        if (g_driver < 0)
        {
                printf("No graphics hardware detected!\n");
                exit(1);
        }

        if (g_mode == CGAHI)
           g_mode = CGAC2;
        initgraph(&g_driver,&g_mode,"");

        setcolor(3);
        settextjustify(CENTER_TEXT,TOP_TEXT);
        settextstyle(GOTHIC_FONT,HORIZ_DIR,1);
        outtextxy(getmaxx()/2,1,"The Graphics Window:");
        rectangle(getmaxx()/20-5,3*getmaxy()/20-5,
                  getmaxx()-getmaxx()/20+5,getmaxy()-getmaxy()/20+5);
        setviewport(getmaxx()/20,3*getmaxy()/20,
                  getmaxx()-getmaxx()/20,getmaxy()-getmaxy()/20,-1);
        MIN_X = 0;
        MIN_Y = 0;
        MAX_X = getmaxx() - getmaxx()/10;
        MAX_Y = getmaxy() - getmaxy()/5;

}

main()
{
     unsigned int i,j,k;
     int x[4] = {30,60,200,200};
     int y[4] = {90,21,145,100};
     int dx[4] = {5,3,7,4};
     int dy[4] = {7,6,5,6};
     int oldx[4][20],oldy[4][20];
     int time;

     printf("Run for how long? ");
     scanf("%d",&time);
     for ( i = 0;  i < 20;  i++ )
        for( j = 0;  j < 4;  j++ )
        {
                oldx[j][i] = 0;
                oldy[j][i] = 0;
        }
     start_graph();

     for ( i=1;  i < time; i++ )
     {
        setcolor(0);
        for ( j = 0;  j < 4;  j++ )
           line(oldx[j][19],oldy[j][19],
                   oldx[(j+1)%4][19],oldy[(j+1)%4][19]);
        setcolor(1);
        for ( j = 0;  j < 4;  j++ )

        line( x[j], y[j], x[(j+1)%4], y[(j+1)%4] );
        for ( j = 0;  j < 4;  j++ )
        {
                if ( x[j]+dx[j] >MAX_X || x[j]+dx[j] < MIN_X )
                   dx[j] *= -1;
                if ( y[j]+dy[j] >MAX_Y || y[j]+dy[j] < MIN_Y )
                   dy[j] *= -1;
```

```
for ( k = 19;  k > 0;  k-- )
{
    oldx[j][k] = oldx[j][k-1];
    oldy[j][k] = oldy[j][k-1];
}
oldx[j][0] = x[j];
oldy[j][0] = y[j];
x[j] += dx[j];
y[j] += dy[j];
}
}
closegraph();
}
```

Only one function is defined: Start_graph( ). This function will prepare the PC for the graphics commands that will be used in the main program. Most of the work is done in main( ).

Two global integer variables are necessary when using the *Turbo C* graphics commands. The variable *g_driver* will contain a number that represents what graphics card is available on your system. The variable *g_mode* will contain the graphics mode that will be used by the graphics system.

In any program that uses graphics, you should start by calling the function detectgraph( ). This function takes two parameters. Both parameters are pointers to integers. You'll place two of the global variables (*g_driver* and *g_mode*) in these parameters. When the function returns to the main program, these variables will contain values. (Here you see an example of a function that returns two different values at the same time by using pointers. The method for doing this is beyond the scope of this book.)

When detectgraph( ) returns, *g_driver* will contain a number representing the type of graphics hardware installed. A list of these numbers appears under the function initgraph( ) in the *Turbo C Additions and Enhancements* update manual that comes with *Turbo C*. This book will be mentioned several times, but it will be referred to simply as the update manual. If you have a new version of *Turbo C* that doesn't include this manual, it may be because these functions have been incorporated into one of the other manuals in a later edition. Please check the index for the function given.

Macros have been defined for each of these drivers, so you need not remember the numbers. These macros appear in the header file graphics.h.

Best graphics mode. The variable *g_mode* will contain the best graphics mode available on the hardware in *g_driver*. *Turbo C* defines *best mode* as the mode with the highest resolution. If you have CGA graphics, for example, *Turbo C* will consider 640 × 200 monochrome graphics better than 320 × 200 color graphics. If you object to the mode chosen by detectgraph( ), it may be changed simply by changing the number in the global variable *g_mode* before graphics are initialized. A list of possible modes also appears in the update manual mentioned above, under the function initgraph( ).

Look at the function start_graph( ) in Figure 18-1. First, detectgraph( ) is called. If this function cannot find any graphics cards, it will place a negative number in *g_driver*. If this variable is negative, the program will print an error message to the screen and call the DOS function exit( ).

Exit( ). Exit( ) is a special function that automatically ends the program. It takes one parameter: a status value. Don't worry too much about this value as it isn't often used. Zero is used to represent a program that is exiting as part of normal operation. When exit( ) returns a value of 1, it represents a program that is exiting because it encountered an error.

Next, the program compares the graphics mode with the value associated with high-resolution CGA graphics (CGAHI). As mentioned before, high-resolution CGA graphics does not use color. Because this program is going to use color, it must downgrade the graphics mode to one that does use color—in this case, CGAC2.

Once the mode is determined, you must actually initialize the graphics. This is done with initgraph( ). This function takes three parameters. The first two are identical to the parameters used with detectgraph( ). The variable *g_driver* must contain a number representing the installed graphics card. The variable *g_mode* must contain the desired graphics mode. These can be determined either by the programmer or by detectgraph( ) as mentioned above. The final parameter is a character string that tells *Turbo C* where the graphics drivers are located. In most cases, you'll simply use a null string (" ") to signify the current working directory.

In the program in Figure 18-1, initgraph( ) uses the driver and mode determined by detectgraph( ). It assumes that the graphics drivers are in the current directory.

Graphics and Text

Now that graphics is initialized, you may start using the *Turbo C* graphics routines. This program will do three different things. First, it will draw a title at the top of the screen. Next, it will draw a border. Once this is done, a shape will be made to bounce around inside the border.

The graphics text functions are quite powerful, allowing text justification and different fonts. Even so, printing text to the screen is a simple proposition. The function outtextxy( ) has three parameters. The first two describe an *x,y* coordinate on the screen. The third parameter contains a character string. Outtextxy( ) will print this text string at the *x,y* coordinates specified by the first two parameters.

The program in Figure 18-1 will print the title *The Graphics Window:* centered at the top of the screen. In order to find the middle of the screen, it uses the function getmaxx( ). This function will return the *x* coordinate of the right edge of the screen. By dividing this by 2, you can obtain the coordinate of the middle of the screen. Note that this function may return different values for different graphics modes. By using getmaxx( ) rather than assuming some value of *x*, the program ensures that the string will appear in the middle of the screen regardless of the hardware. The outtextxy( ) command looks like this:

```
outtextxy(getmaxx( )/2,1,"The Graphics Window:");
```

Outtextxy( ) always uses the current text color, style, and justification. The above statement works, but this program will appear fancier if you use different fonts and colors. Changing the color is the simplest. Setcolor( ) takes one parameter, an integer that stands for a color. The number of colors varies with the graphics mode. This program will play it safe and assume only four colors exist.

After graphics are initialized, the program in Figure 18-1 changes the current color to color 3 (which is brown in mode CGAC2) and uses the function settextjustify( ) to change the current justification of text. This function takes two parameters, the horizontal justification and the vertical justification. Possible values for these settings are shown in the update manual under the gettextsettings( ) function.

This program uses CENTER_TEXT to cause text to be centered around the print location in the horizontal direction and uses TOP_TEXT to cause text to be printed below the print location in the vertical direction.

After the justification is set, the function settextstyle( ) is used to choose the font in which to draw the text. This function has three parameters:

- Font
- Direction
- Character size

The basic fonts are listed in the update manual mentioned above, under the function gettextsettings( ). They are defined as macros in the graphics.h header file. Two directions may be chosen. HORIZ_DIR causes all text to be printed horizontally from left to right. VERT_DIR causes all text to be printed vertically from bottom to top (the text is rotated counterclockwise 90 degrees).

The program in Figure 18-1 will print text to the screen horizontally in the Gothic font. Text is only printed in one place in the program, but if any other text had been printed, it would appear using the same style and justification.

Line Graphics and Viewports

After the title is written, a rectangular border is drawn on the screen. This is done using the rectangle( ) function. This function takes four parameters. These parameters hold the coordinates of the left, top, right, and bottom edges in that order. Although this appears to be very simple, you may be confused about how the function is called in this program. What follows is an explanation of the procedure.

The rectangle should fill the screen, leaving a small border area and a slightly larger array for the text that was printed above. Unfortunately, because the graphics hardware (and therefore the graphics mode) may vary, you cannot be sure that a given set of values will work on any machine. If you used a specific set of values, your program would only work on machines exactly like yours, using the same hardware as yours. The solution to this problem is to use the getmaxx( ) and getmaxy( ) functions. These functions will always return the size of the screen in pixels. (A pixel is a single dot on the graphics screen.)

To find the border of the screen, the program takes the maximum coordinates of the screen and divides them by 20. The border rectangle will actually be slightly larger than this, so 5 is either added or subtracted depending on the size of the screen. Now you only need to make room for the text graphics at the top. This is done by making the border three times as large as normal. This gives the following four coordinates:

$$3 * \text{getmaxy}(\ )-5$$

getmaxx( )−5

getmaxx( )+5

getmaxy( )+5

All graphics will now be drawn inside this rectangle. This is done by using setviewport( ). This command works in a manner similar to the textwindow( ) function. Setviewport( ) takes five parameters. The first four parameters are identical to those used by rectangle( ). They specify the rectangle in which to draw all graphics. The fifth parameter is called the clipping flag. If this flag is true, no graphics will be printed outside of the viewport. If it is false, some graphics may "spill out" of this rectangle.

In the program shown in Figure 18-1, four variables, *MIN_X, MIN_Y, MAX_X*, and *MAX_Y* are used to store the maximum coordinates of the window. Because the corner of the viewport is now 0,0, the variables *MIN_Y* and *MIN_X* are set to 0. For the same reason, *MAX_X* and *MAX_Y* must be reduced to account for both borders. These global variables will be used in the main program.

The Main Program

What will this program do? The program will keep track of four points on the screen in a large loop. Each time the program runs through this loop, lines will be drawn between the given points. These lines will be left on the screen for 20 iterations and then will be removed.

First, the program creates two arrays to hold the *x,y* co-ordinates of the four points. These are called *x* and *y*. These arrays are initialized in a special way:

int x[4] = {30,60,200,200};

You can initialize an array by setting it equal to a set of numbers enclosed in brackets. The above statement will place 30 in *x[0]*, 60 in *x[1]*, 200 in *x[2]*, and 200 in *x[3]*.

Next, the program must keep track of how fast each of the points is moving. The speed is represented by a small integer which may be positive or negative. These integers are added to the *x,y* coordinates to produce new *x,y* coordinates. There must be a speed for each coordinate so the program creates two more arrays of four integers called *dx* and *dy*. Values in *dx* represent speeds of the various points in the horizontal direction; *dy* represents speeds in the vertical direction.

Finally, because the program must erase lines after they have been on the screen for 20 iterations, the program must store the last 20 sets of points. This is done with a new kind of array: a two-dimensional array.

Two-dimensional array. A two-dimensional array is similar to a standard array except that each element has two indices rather than one. In a sense, a two-dimensional array can be thought of as an "array of arrays." The program must keep track of 20 sets of four *x,y* coordinates. One set of *x* coordinates are stored in an array of four integers. Twenty sets of *x* coordinates are stored in an array of 20 arrays of four integers. Such an array might be declared like this:

```
int oldx[4][20];
```

In this declaration, the first index represents the point number 0–3. The second index represents how old that point is, from 0–19 iterations old.

Running the program. These are the data structures that will be used in the main program. Now look at the executable portion of the code in Figure 18-1. First, the program prompts the user for an integer representing the amount of time to run the program. Next, the elements of *oldx* and *oldy* are initialized to 0 in a nested *for* loop. (You could have done this in the declaration, but you would have had to place 800 zeros within the braces.) The function startgraph( ) is then used to initialize the graphics routines, draw the border and set the viewport.

The rest of the program is contained in a *for* loop. The amount of time that this loop will run depends on the value entered by the user at the beginning. Each time through this loop, the program performs the series of actions outlined below.

First, the program sets the color to 0 (black) and erases the lines in the last position in the arrays *oldx* and *oldy* using the function line( ). This will always be the oldest set of lines. Line( ) takes four parameters. These parameters represent two pairs of *x,y* coordinates. Line( ) will draw a line between these two points in the current color—in this case, black.

Next, the program sets the color to 1 and draws four lines connecting the four points stored in *x* and *y*. First, point 0 is connected to point 1. Then, point 1 is connected to point 2, point 2 to point 3, and finally, point 3 is connected back to point 0. This is accomplished with the modulus operator. If *j* is less than 3, then (j+1)%4 is the same as *j+1* (1%4 = 1, 2%4 = 2, 3%4 = 3). If *j* is equal to 3, then (j+1)%4 is equal to 0 (4%4=0). This allows the program to easily wrap values around without special *if* statements.

At this point, four lines have been drawn on the screen. Now the program determines where to draw the next set of lines. First, it takes each *x* coordinate (in *x*) and adds the speed value (in *dx*) to it. If this value would place the point off the screen, the speed value is multiplied by −1, causing the point to move in the opposite direction and making it appear to bounce off the edge of the screen. The same is done for the *y* coordinates. The actual values of *x* and *y* are not changed at this point.

Next, the current values of *x* and *y* must be saved to the arrays *oldx* and *oldy*. Before this can be done, space must be cleared to make room for them. This is done in a *for* loop that moves every value in each of these arrays up one element. The values of *x* and *y* then are stored at the bottom of this chain. The variables *x* and *y* then are updated to their new positions by adding the values in *dx* and *dy* to them.

When the loop starts again, new lines will be drawn corresponding to the new values of *x* and *y*. In addition, the lines stored at the end of the chain will be erased. These lines represent lines originally drawn 20 iterations ago.

When the loop ends, one final function is called. The function closegraph( ) will return your machine to text mode.

Compiling Graphics Programs

To compile any program using graphics, you must create a special project file. All graphics routines are contained in a file called graphics.lib. These routines must be linked with the rest of the program. For this program, this can be done by setting up a simple project file with the following two entries:

```
graph.c
graphics.lib
```

Then place the program listed in Figure 18-1 in a file called graph.c and compile this project. If you don't link in graphics.lib, *Turbo C* will not be able to find any of the graphics routines.

Try running this program. As you can see, sophisticated graphics can be drawn with little effort. Of course, as with any kind of art, it's much easier to draw random shapes than pictures of actual objects. Given time and patience, virtually anything can be drawn using computer graphics.

You'll probably want to experiment with this program to see what else can be done. This program only used a few graphics functions. There are actually a large number of them. Circles can be drawn with ellipse( ), and portions of circles can be drawn with arc( ). These and other functions are similar to the functions shown in this chapter, and you should have little trouble using them.

Summary
In the process of writing a brief graphics program, this chapter contained information on how to determine through software the graphics capabilities of your computer, text on the high-resolution screen, viewports, and line graphics. You also saw one application for a two-dimensional array. Finally, there was a brief mention of the requirements to compile a graphics program.

Chapter 19
The Game

Games are usually thought of as a simple, somewhat frivolous application for computers. But, in fact, a good game can be one of the most difficult programs to write. This chapter contains a very simple poker-playing program and, as you'll see, it is by far the most complicated program in this book. The programs in the previous two chapters were not large enough to justify splitting them into separate files. The poker-playing program in this chapter contains 21 different functions and is separated into two main files (and some header files).

The Data Structures

In any program, the first task is to define the data structures the program uses. In this case, you need to define structures that are able to store playing cards. This is done in the header file poker.h (shown in Figure 19-1).

Figure 19-1. Header File poker.h

```
/*poker.h*/
#include <alloc.h>
#include <conio.h>
#include <stdio.h>
#define ACE 14
#define TWO 2
#define THREE 3
#define FOUR 4
#define FIVE 5
#define SIX 6
#define SEVEN 7
#define EIGHT 8
#define NINE 9
#define TEN 10
#define JACK 11
#define QUEEN 12
#define KING 13
#define SPADES 1
#define DIAMONDS 2
#define HEARTS 3
#define CLUBS 4
#define SHUFFLE_LENGTH 10000
#define TRUE -1
#define FALSE 0
#define VAL_ZIP 0
#define VAL_TWO_KIND 1
#define VAL_TWO_PAIR 2
```

```
#define VAL_THREE_KIND 3
#define VAL_STRAIGHT 4
#define VAL_FULL_HOUSE 5
#define VAL_FLUSH 6
#define VAL_FOUR_KIND 7
#define VAL_STRAIGHT_FLUSH 8
#define GETXY() gotoxy(xwin1,ywin1);
#define STOREXY() xwin1 = wherex(); ywin1 = wherey();
#define WINDOW1() window(1,16,80,25); textcolor(CYAN);
#define WINDOW2() window(1,5,40,13); textcolor(GREEN);
#define WINDOW3() window(41,5,60,13); textcolor(RED) ;
#define WINDOW4() window(20,3,40,4); textcolor(MAGENTA);


typedef char suit;
typedef char rank;

typedef struct
{
        rank card_rank;
        suit card_suit;

} card;

typedef struct
{
        rank card1,card2;
        int value;

} card_value;

typedef struct
{
        rank hand_rank[5];
        suit hand_suit[5];

} hand;
```

First, to help improve program readability, each rank and suit is assigned a number. The different possible values that can be held in a hand of five cards are also assigned numbers.

This program will also use windows so the window routines have been copied directly from the database example in Chapter 17. In addition, two new routines, GETXY( ) and STOREXY( ) have been added. These will be described in more detail later.

First, the variable types suit and rank are declared as being type char. This is used merely to make the program more readable. It makes it more obvious whether a variable is supposed to hold a rank or a suit.

Next, a structure called *card* is created that contains both a rank and a suit. This structure will be used to hold single cards.

Next, a structure called *card_value* is created. This will contain the ranking of a hand. The *value* field will contain one of the values listed in the macros section. The two ranks are used to store the ranks of cards in that hand. For instance, if you have a full house, it's important to know what cards make up the full house. The use of this structure will become more clear later on.

Finally, a structure called *hand* is created. This structure holds both the ranks and suits of five cards.

The chkhand.c File

The rest of the program is split into two files. The main file, poker.c, contains main( ) as well as other code related to the game itself. This file will be discussed later. The file chkhand.c contains a number of routines that compare hands with each other. In order for a poker-playing program to work, the program must be able to evaluate a hand of five cards and compare two hands to determine a winner.

The first function puts the hand in sorted order. As you'll see, it's much easier to determine the value of a hand if it has been sorted in rank order. Sorting can be a very complicated proposition. Fortunately, because only five cards must be sorted, a very simple sort function can be used. It appears in Figure 19-2.

Figure 19-2. Sort Function

```
sort(the_hand)
hand *the_hand;
{
        int i,j;
        char temp;

        for(i=0;i<4;i++)
                for(j=i+1;j<5;j++)
                        if(the_hand->hand_rank[i]<the_hand->hand_rank[j])
                        {

                                temp = the_hand->hand_rank[j];
                                the_hand->hand_rank[j] = the_hand->hand_rank[i];
                                the_hand->hand_rank[i] = temp;
                                temp = the_hand->hand_suit[j];
                                the_hand->hand_suit[j] = the_hand->hand_suit[i];
                                the_hand->hand_suit[i] = temp;
                        }
}
```

This function takes a pointer to a hand (defined in poker.h) and sorts that hand. Because the parameter is a pointer, there is no need to return anything. By modifying the object that the pointer points to, you're modifying that object in the main program as well.

The way this function works is simple. It looks at the first card and compares it with the card above it. If the card above it has a lower rank, the two cards are swapped. The first card is then compared with the third card. If this card is lower, the two cards are swapped. This continues up to the end of the hand. At this point, you know that the lowest card must be in the first location. The process repeats, this time starting with the second card. Now the first two cards are in sorted order. The process then repeats with the third card. Finally, the fourth card is compared to the fifth card. Once this has been done, the cards will be in sorted order.

Notice that when two cards are to be swapped, both the *hand_rank* and *hand_suit* fields must be swapped. Whenever you're sorting structures, you must remember to swap all portions of that structure.

Evaluation functions. After sort( ), a large group of evaluation functions appears in this file. The purpose of each of these functions is similar. One function exists for each possible hand value. Each function takes a hand pointer and returns a flag. If the hand passed to the function has that value, a rank is returned, otherwise a value of false is returned.

Consider the straight( ) function in Figure 19-3.

Figure 19-3. straight( )

```
straight(the_hand)
hand *the_hand;
{
        if(the_hand->hand_rank[0] == the_hand->hand_rank[1] +1 &&
           the_hand->hand_rank[1] == the_hand->hand_rank[2] +1 &&
           the_hand->hand_rank[2] == the_hand->hand_rank[3] +1 &&
           the_hand->hand_rank[3] == the_hand->hand_rank[4] +1)
                return the_hand->hand_rank[0];
        if(the_hand->hand_rank[4] == TWO && the_hand->hand_rank[0] == ACE &&
           the_hand->hand_rank[1] == the_hand->hand_rank[2] +1 &&
           the_hand->hand_rank[2] == the_hand->hand_rank[3] +1 &&
           the_hand->hand_rank[0] == the_hand->hand_rank[1] +1)
                return ACE;
        return FALSE;
}
```

This function will receive a sorted hand as a parameter and consists of two conditional statements. The first statement compares each card with the card after it. If each rank is exactly 1 more than the rank after it, then the hand is a straight, and the value of the first card is returned.

An ace may be either the first or the last card in a straight, so a second conditional statement is necessary. This is almost identical to the first, except that if the last card (the lowest because of sorting) is a 2, and the first card (the highest) is an ace, and the rest of the cards comprise a straight, then the condition is true. In this case, the rank ace is returned. If both these conditions fail, false is returned to signify that no straight was found.

The next function, flush( ) (Figure 19-4), returns a value of true if all the values of the *hand_suit* field are equal. If this is not the case, it returns false.

Figure 19-4. flush( )

```
flush(the_hand)
hand *the_hand;
{
        if(the_hand->hand_suit[0] == the_hand->hand_suit[1] &&
           the_hand->hand_suit[1] == the_hand->hand_suit[2] &&
           the_hand->hand_suit[2] == the_hand->hand_suit[3] &&
           the_hand->hand_suit[3] == the_hand->hand_suit[4])
                return TRUE;
        return FALSE;
}
```

The four_kind( ) function (Figure 19-5) looks at the first card, comparing it with the next three. If the ranks are all equal, the function returns the value of that card. If not, it looks at the second card, comparing this with the next three. Again, if they are all equal, the function returns the value of the card. Note that this function is simplified by the fact that the cards are in sorted order. Cards of equal rank must be next to each other. Again, if all tests fail, a value of false is returned.

Figure 19-5. four_kind( )

```
four_kind(the_hand)
hand *the_hand;
{
        int i;

        for(i=0;i<2;i++)
                if(the_hand->hand_rank[i] == the_hand->hand_rank[i+1] &&
                   the_hand->hand_rank[i+1] == the_hand->hand_rank[i+2] &&
                   the_hand->hand_rank[i+2] == the_hand->hand_rank[i+3])
                        return the_hand->hand_rank[i];
        return FALSE;
}
```

The three_kind( ) function (Figure 19-6) is almost identical to four_kind( ). The first card is compared to the next two
cards. If they have equal rank, the card rank is returned. This
is done again with the second and third cards. A value of false
is returned if the hand does not contain three of a kind.

Figure 19-6. three_kind( )

```
three_kind(the_hand)
hand *the_hand;
{
        int i;

        for(i=0;i<3;i++)
                if(the_hand->hand_rank[i] == the_hand->hand_rank[i+1] &&
                   the_hand->hand_rank[i+1] == the_hand->hand_rank[i+2])
                        return the_hand->hand_rank[i];
        return FALSE;
}
```

The two_kind( ) function (Figure 19-7) is similar to the
previous two functions. Each card is compared with its succes-
sor. If any two cards are the same, the card value is returned.
Otherwise a value of false is returned.

Figure 19-7. two_kind( )

```
two_kind(the_hand)
hand *the_hand;
{
        int i;

        for(i=0;i<4;i++)
                if(the_hand->hand_rank[i] == the_hand->hand_rank[i+1])
                        return the_hand->hand_rank[i];
        return FALSE;
}
```

The function shown in Figure 19-8, two_pair( ), is a little
trickier. First, the function looks for a pair. If one is found,
then the remaining cards are examined for another pair. If another pair is found, and the rank of the cards in the second
pair is not the same as the first pair, the rank of the second
pair is returned (this will be important later).

Figure 19-8. two_pair( )

```
two_pair(the_hand)
hand *the_hand;
{
        int i,j;

        for(i=0;i<2;i++)
                if(the_hand->hand_rank[i] == the_hand->hand_rank[i+1])
                        for(j=i+2;j<4;j++)
                                if(the_hand->hand_rank[j] == the_hand->hand_rank[j+1] &&
                                   the_hand->hand_rank[j] != the_hand->hand_rank[i])
                                        return the_hand->hand_rank[j];
        return FALSE;
}
```

The final function, full_house( ) (Figure 19-9), is fairly simple. A full house can exist in two ways. Either the first three cards are equal to each other and the second two are equal to each other, or the first two cards are equal and the last three cards are equal. If this is the case, then the rank of the three equal cards is returned.

Figure 19-9. full_house( )

```
full_house(the_hand)
hand *the_hand;
{
        int i,j;
        if(the_hand->hand_rank[0] == the_hand->hand_rank[1] &&
           the_hand->hand_rank[2] == the_hand->hand_rank[3] &&
           the_hand->hand_rank[3] == the_hand->hand_rank[4])
                return the_hand->hand_rank[3];
        if(the_hand->hand_rank[0] == the_hand->hand_rank[1] &&
           the_hand->hand_rank[1] == the_hand->hand_rank[2] &&
           the_hand->hand_rank[3] == the_hand->hand_rank[4])
                return the_hand->hand_rank[3];
        return FALSE;
}
```

There are two more functions in chkhnd.c. The first, eval_hand( ), takes a *hand* as a parameter and returns its value in a pointer to a *hand_value*. It does this with a complicated set of conditionals. The *hand_value* that is returned will contain an integer representing the value of the hand as well as possibly one or two card ranks. This value will be used by the last function to compare two hands.

First, the function creates the variable *card_val* and reserves space for it. Then it checks to see if the hand is a straight with the straight( ) function. If it is, it checks for a flush. If the hand is also a flush, the function sets the value of the hand to a straight flush and stores the low card in the *card1* field. This value will be used if more than one hand contains a straight flush. In this case, the higher straight will win. If the hand is not a flush, then the function sets the value to straight.

If the hand was not a straight, the function checks for a flush. If the hand is a flush, the function returns the value for a flush; otherwise, it continues on.

The function continues on through the various types of hands. It looks for the highest values first, only looking for lower values if a higher value is not found. If nothing at all is found, then the card value is set to *val_zip* to represent nothing found. The flow of the entire function is described in Figure 19-10.

Figure 19-10. Poker-Playing Program Flow

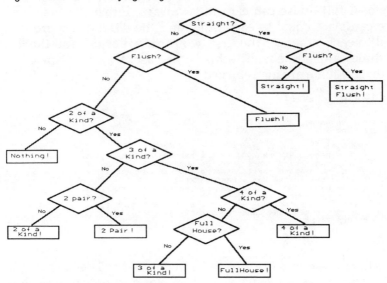

In some case, ranks of two cards must be assigned to the structure. For example, if you have two pair, you need to determine the ranks of both pairs. Because of the way the evaluation functions were written, this is not difficult. If two pair are found, both two_pair( ) and two_kind( ) are called. Two_kind( ) will always return the rank of the first pair it finds. Two_pair( ) always returns the rank of the second. Buy calling both, the function is able to determine the values of both pairs.

The last function in chkhand.c, compare_hand (Figure 19-11), compares two hands. If the first of the two hands is better, it returns true. Otherwise, it returns false.

This function is quite simple. First, it evaluates both hands with eval_hand( ). If the value of the first is higher than the second, a value of true is returned. If the values are equal, then the ranks in the value structure are compared. If the first hand has the greater rank, true is returned. If the second hand has the greater rank, false is returned. If these ranks are equal, then the second rank field in the value structure must be checked. If both hands contain the same rank in this field also, then each card in one hand is compared individually with the corresponding card in the other hand. As soon as a pair of cards fails to match, victory is assigned to the hand with the higher card.

As you know, the *rank* field of the value structure may contain nothing. For example, if a flush is found, neither *rank* field is assigned anything. These fields are each initialized to 1. The only time these fields are compared is if the same hand value is found. In such a case, the rank fields for both hands will contain 1's which the function will see as equal.

The whole purpose of this file is the three functions sort( ), eval—hand( ), and compare—hand( ). The main program will not use any of the other functions in this file.

Figure 19-11. compare—hand

```
card_value *eval_hand(the_hand)
hand *the_hand;
{
        card_value *card_val;

        card_val = (card_value *)malloc(sizeof(card_val));
        card_val->card1 = 1;
        card_val->card2 = 1;
        if(straight(the_hand))
                if(flush(the_hand))
                        if(the_hand->hand_rank[0] == JACK)
                                card_val->value = VAL_STRAIGHT_FLUSH;
                        else
                        {
                                card_val->value = VAL_STRAIGHT_FLUSH;
                                card_val->card1 = the_hand->hand_rank[0];
                        }
                else
                {
                        card_val->value = VAL_STRAIGHT;
                        card_val->card1 = the_hand->hand_rank[0];
                }
        else
                if(flush(the_hand))
                        card_val->value = VAL_FLUSH;
        else
        if(two_kind(the_hand))
                if(three_kind(the_hand))
                        if(four_kind(the_hand))
                        {
                                card_val->value = VAL_FOUR_KIND;
                                card_val->card1 = four_kind(the_hand);
                        }
                        else
                                if(full_house(the_hand))
                                {
                                        card_val->value = VAL_FULL_HOUSE;
                                        card_val->card1 = two_kind(the_hand);
                                        card_val->card2 = full_house(the_hand);
                                }
                                else
                                {
                                        card_val->value = VAL_THREE_KIND;
                                        card_val->card1 = three_kind(the_hand);
                                }
                        else
                        if(two_pair(the_hand))
                        {
                                card_val->value = VAL_TWO_PAIR;
                                card_val->card1 = two_kind(the_hand);
                                card_val->card2 = two_pair(the_hand);
                        }
                else
                {
```

```
                        card_val->value = VAL_TWO_KIND;
                        card_val->card1 = two_kind(the_hand);
                }
        else
                card_val->value = VAL_ZIP;
        return card_val;
}

int compare_hand(hand1,hand2)
hand * hand1,* hand2;
{
        card_value *val1,*val2;
        int i;

        val1=eval_hand(hand1);
        val2=eval_hand(hand2);
        if(val1->value > val2->value)
                return TRUE;
        if(val1->value == val2->value)
        {
                if(val1->card1 > val2->card1)
                        return TRUE;
                if(val1->card1 < val2->card1)
                        return FALSE;
                if(val1->card2 > val2->card2)
                        return TRUE;
                if(val1->card2 < val2->card2)
                        return FALSE;
                for(i=0;i<5;i++)
                {
                        if(hand1->hand_rank[i]>hand2->hand_rank[i])
                                return TRUE;
                        if(hand1->hand_rank[i]<hand2->hand_rank[i])
                                return FALSE;
                }
        }
        return FALSE;
}
```

The poker.c File

The file poker.c contains the rest of the program. Some new data structures are defined, and a number of routines exist to handle the mechanics of the poker game itself.

Examine the declarations in Figure 19-12. First, two arrays of strings are declared containing the names of the different suits and ranks. These arrays ease the task of printing cards to the screen. Next the program declares an array of 52 cards. This will be the deck of cards.

The first function in poker.c is called init_deck( ) (Figure 19-13). This function sets up the initial deck of cards using a simple *for* loop. After this function exits, the deck array will contain all 52 cards in sorted order.

Figure 19-12. Declarations in poker.c

```
/* poker.c */
#include "poker.h"
#define case_rank(X) case X : cprintf("%s",rank_name[X]); break;
#define case_suit(X) case X : cprintf("%s",suit_name[X]); break;

char rank_name[15][10] = {"BLANK","Blank","Two","Three","Four","Five","Six",
                          "Seven","Eight","Nine","Ten","Jack","Queen","King",
                          "Ace"};

char suit_name[5][10] = {"Blank","Spades","Diamonds","Hearts","Clubs"};

card deck[52];
int top_card=1;

void show_hand(hand *);
hand *deal_hand(void);
void init_deck(void);
void shuffle(void);
void print_value(card_value *);
card_value *eval_hand(hand *);

#include "chkhnd.c"
#include "pause.c"
```

Figure 19-13. init_deck( )

```
void init_deck()
{

        int i,j;
        for(i=0;i<13;i++)
                for(j=0;j<4;j++)
                {

                        deck[i*4+j].card_rank=i+2;
                        deck[i*4+j].card_suit=j+1;

                }

}
```

The next function (Figure 19-14) is used to shuffle the hand. This function works by picking two cards at random and swapping them. This is done 10,000 times (this number can be increased or reduced by changing the value of the constant *SHUFFLE_LENGTH*). Random cards are chosen using the function rand( ). This function returns a random number between 0 and 32,767. To narrow this range to the range of possible cards, the modulus operator is used. The subexpression *rand( ) % 52* will return a number between 0 and 51. This exactly corresponds to the indices of *deck*. In addition, the global variable *top_card* is set to 0. This represents the top card on the deck.

Figure 19-14. shuffle( )

```
void shuffle()
{
                int i;
                char card1,card2;
                card temp_card;

                top_card = 0;
                cprintf("Shuffling");
                for(i=0;i<SHUFFLE_LENGTH;i++)
                {
                        if(i%1000 == 0)
                                cprintf(".");
                        card1 = rand() % 52;
                        card2 = rand() % 52;
                        temp_card = deck[card1];
                        deck[card1] = deck[card2];
                        deck[card2] = temp_card;

                }
                cprintf("\n");

}
```

The next function, draw—card( ), shown in Figure 19-15, will draw a card from the deck and place it in a player's hand. It takes two parameters: a pointer to the hand to place the card in and the position in that hand where the card is to be placed. This function takes the *rank* and *suit* on the top of the deck and places them in the correct fields in the hand. The variable *top—card* is then incremented so that card cannot be chosen again. Finally, the hand pointer is returned. Note that if the deck has been exhausted, an error message is printed, and −1 is returned.

Figure 19-15. draw—card( )

```
hand *draw_card(the_hand,the_card)
hand *the_hand;
int the_card;
{
            if(top_card >= 52)
            {
                    cprintf("Error! No more cards!");
                    return (hand *) -1;

            }
            the_hand->hand_rank[the_card] = deck[top_card].card_rank;
            the_hand->hand_suit[the_card] = deck[top_card++].card_suit;
            return the_hand;
}
```

After draw—card( ) comes deal—hand( ) (Figure 19-16). This routine uses draw—card( ) to fill a five-card hand. First it allocates space for the hand and then it calls draw—card( ) for each position in the hand. Note that if draw—card( ) returns −1, this will be passed on by deal—hand( ).

Figure 19-16. deal—hand( )

```
hand *deal_hand()
{
        char ch,card;
        int i;
        hand *the_hand;

        the_hand = (hand *) malloc(sizeof(hand));

        for(i=0;i<5;i++)
                the_hand = draw_card(the_hand,i);
        return the_hand;

}
```

A more complicated function is ask—then—draw( ) (Figure 19-17). This function asks the user which cards to redraw and then uses draw—card( ) to replace only those cards. This is done by reading a string from the keyboard. Only the first five characters of this string are used. These characters are checked one by one. Wherever a 1 is found in this string, a card is drawn and placed in the corresponding position in the hand; otherwise, the card in that position is left alone. Thus, if the user entered 11000, the first two cards in the hand would be replaced. The function will then return a pointer to the hand.

Figure 19-17. ask—then—draw( )

```
hand *ask_then_draw(the_hand)
hand *the_hand;
{
        int i;
        char tmpstr[10];
        cprintf("Draw which cards? (ex. 10101 draws 1,3,5)");
        gets(tmpstr);
        cprintf("\n\n");
        for(i=0;i<5;i++)
        {
                if(tmpstr[i] == '1')
                the_hand = draw_card(the_hand,i);
        }
        return the_hand;

}
```

The function show_hand( ) (Figure 19-18) prints the contents of a hand to the screen.

Figure 19-18. show_hand( )

```
void show_hand(the_hand)
hand *the_hand;
{
        char ch,card;
        int i;
        for(i=0;i<5;i++)
        {
            print_card(the_hand->hand_rank[i],the_hand->hand_suit[i]);
        }

}
```

Most of the work is done by the function print_card( ) shown in Figure 19-19. The print_card( ) function takes two parameters, a *rank* and a *suit*. It takes these variables and prints the corresponding strings. This is done in two switch statements. Each of these switch statements contains a special kind of function called a macro function.

Figure 19-19. print_card

```
print_card(crank,csuit)
rank crank;
suit csuit;
{
        switch(crank)
        {
                case_rank(TWO);
                case_rank(THREE);
                case_rank(FOUR);
                case_rank(FIVE);
                case_rank(SIX);
                case_rank(SEVEN);
                case_rank(EIGHT);
                case_rank(NINE);
                case_rank(TEN);
                case_rank(JACK);
                case_rank(QUEEN);
                case_rank(KING);
                case_rank(ACE);
                default : cprintf("%d",crank);
        }
        cprintf(" Of ");
        switch(csuit)
        {
                case_suit(SPADES);
                case_suit(DIAMONDS);
                case_suit(HEARTS);
                case_suit(CLUBS);
                default : cprintf("%d",csuit);
        }
        cprintf("\n");
}
```

Macros are standard definitions with parameters. Two macro functions are defined in Figure 19-20.

Figure 19-20. Two Defined Macro Statements

```
#define case_rank(X) case X : cprintf("%s",rank_name[X]); break;
#define case_suit(X) case X : cprintf("%s",suit_name[X]); break;
```

The text that makes up the macro is replaced by its definition, with parameters substituted at the appropriate place. For example, we could create a macro called square:

#define square(x) (x) * (x)

Later on in the program, we could use the macro like this:

b = square(a);

Before the program is compiled, the definition for the macro would be substituted everywhere the macro is used, resulting in this:

b = (a) * (a);

In this program, *case_rank(THREE)* would become the following:

```
case THREE : cprintf("%s",rank_name[THREE]); break;
```

By using the macros in Figure 19-20, you can save yourself a great deal of typing in print_card( ).

If you understand how these macros work, you should have little trouble understanding print_card( ). It simply contains two case statements, using the arrays *rank_name* and *suit_name* to map the integer value of a rank or suit to the appropriate string.

For a poker game to be enjoyable, you need an opponent. The function pick_then_draw( ) (Figure 19-21) allows the computer to act as an intelligent opponent. First, the function will evaluate the hand. Then it will determine which cards should be discarded. It will then call draw_card( ) to replace these cards.

Figure 19-21. pick_then_draw( )

```
hand *pick_then_draw(the_hand)
hand *the_hand;
{
        card_value *card_val;
        int drawn = 0,i;

        card_val = eval_hand(the_hand);
        switch(card_val->value)
        {
                case VAL_STRAIGHT :
                case VAL_FLUSH :
                case VAL_STRAIGHT_FLUSH :
                case VAL_FULL_HOUSE :
                                break;
                case VAL_FOUR_KIND :
                case VAL_THREE_KIND :
                case VAL_TWO_KIND :
                        for(i=0;i<5;i++)
                           if(the_hand->hand_rank[i] != card_val->card1)
                           {
                                drawn++;
                                the_hand = draw_card(the_hand,i);
                           }
                        break;
                case VAL_TWO_PAIR :
                        for(i=0;i<5;i++)
                           if(the_hand->hand_rank[i] != card_val->card1 &&
                              the_hand->hand_rank[i] != card_val->card2)
                           {
                                drawn++;
                                the_hand = draw_card(the_hand,i);
                           }
                                        break;
                        default :
                                for(i=2;i<5;i++)
                                        the_hand = draw_card(the_hand,i);
                                drawn=3;

        }
        if(drawn !=0)
                cprintf("I drew %d cards\n",drawn);
        else
                cprintf("I drew 1 card\n");
        return the_hand;
}
```

This function is fairly simple. First, eval_hand( ) is used to determine the value of the hand. Next, the function uses a switch statement to choose the correct course of action. Certain hands, such as straights and flushes, should never be broken up. If any of these is seen, no cards are drawn. If there is one set of matching cards (two, three, or four of a kind), all cards not belonging to that set are replaced using draw_card( ). If two pairs are seen, the card not belonging to either pair is discarded. If the hand is worthless (the default case), then the three worst cards are replaced with draw_card( ). The variable *drawn* is used to report the number of cards drawn to the user.

The final function, print_val( ) (Figure 19-22), uses a simple switch statement to report the value of a hand. Again, a simple case statement is used to map values in the value structure to the English equivalent.

Figure 19-22. print_val( )

```
        void print_val(card_val)
card_value *card_val;
{
        switch(card_val->value)
        {
                case VAL_FLUSH : cprintf("Flush\n");
                                        break;
                case VAL_STRAIGHT : cprintf("Straight\n");
                                        break;
                case VAL_STRAIGHT_FLUSH : if(card_val->card1 != TEN)
                                                cprintf("Straight Flush\n");
                                          else
                                                cprintf("Royal Flush\n");
                                        break;
                case VAL_FULL_HOUSE : cprintf("Full House\n");
                                        break;
                case VAL_FOUR_KIND : cprintf("Four of a Kind\n");
                                        break;
                case VAL_THREE_KIND : cprintf("Three of a Kind\n");
                                        break;
                case VAL_TWO_KIND : cprintf("Two of a Kind\n");
                                        break;
                case VAL_TWO_PAIR : cprintf("Two pair\n");
                                        break;
                default : cprintf("Nothing\n");
        }

}
```

The Main Program

The main( ) function (Figure 19-23) is fairly straightforward.
First, the screen is cleared and some text is drawn to delineate
the windows. Next, the function init_deck( ) is used to initialize the deck of cards.

Figure 19-23. main( )

```
main()
{
    int i=0,his_score=0,my_score=0;
    int xwin1 = 1, ywin1 = 1;
    char ch;
    hand *my_hand,*his_hand;
        unsigned seed;

    textmode(C80);
    textcolor(LIGHTGRAY);
        clrscr();
    cprintf("\n");
    cprintf("                        ,           Score:\n");
    cprintf("    Your Hand                              My Hand\n");
    cprintf("----------------                      ----------------\n");
    cprintf("\n\n\n\n\n\n\n\n\n-----------------------------------------
    init_deck();
    do
    {
            WINDOW2();
            clrscr();
            WINDOW3();
            clrscr();
            WINDOW1();
            clrscr();
            shuffle();
            cprintf("Game %d:\n",++i);
            my_hand = deal_hand();
            sort(my_hand);
            his_hand = deal_hand();
            sort(his_hand);
            STOREXY();
            WINDOW2();
            clrscr();
```

247

```
show_hand(my_hand);
cprintf("\n");
print_val(eval_hand(my_hand));
WINDOW3();
his_hand = pick_then_draw(his_hand);
sort(his_hand);
WINDOW1();
GETXY();
my_hand = ask_then_draw(my_hand);
STOREXY();
WINDOW2();
clrscr();
sort(my_hand);
show_hand(my_hand);
cprintf("\n");
print_val(eval_hand(my_hand));
WINDOW1();
GETXY();
pause();
STOREXY();
WINDOW3();
clrscr();
show_hand(his_hand);
cprintf("\n");
print_val(eval_hand(his_hand));
WINDOW1();
ywin1--;
GETXY();
textcolor(CYAN+BLINK);
if(compare_hand(my_hand,his_hand))
{
     my_score++;
     cprintf("You win!!                    \n");
}
else
{
     his_score++;
     cprintf("I win!!                      \n");
}
STOREXY();
WINDOW4();
clrscr();
cprintf("%d      to      %d\n",my_score,his_score);
WINDOW1();
GETXY();
cprintf("Hit q to quit, any other key to continue.");
ch = getch();
}
while(ch != 'q' && ch != 'Q');
}
```

The main program consists of a large *do* loop. At the end
of this loop, the user will be asked whether the game should
be ended. The loop will end when the user chooses to quit.

First, the program clears the main windows, shuffles the
cards, and prints a game number. Next, it deals two hands: one
for the user *(my_hand)* and one for the computer *(his_hand)*.
These hands are then sorted so that the evaluation routines
will work correctly.

The program uses the macro STOREXY( ) in poker.h to
save the current cursor position in the variables *xwin* and *ywin*
using the functions wherey( ) and wherex( ). As you'll see, the
saved cursor position will be important when the program returns to this window.

Once the cursor is saved, the program switches to window 2 and prints the current hand. It evaluates the hand, printing the results of the evaluation. It then switches to window 3 and uses the function pick_then_draw( ) to choose a plan of action for the computer. The number of cards drawn by the computer is reported (though the values are not).

Next, the program switches back to window 1. Whenever you switch windows, the cursor is automatically placed in the upper left corner. In all previous cases, this has been acceptable as the window was immediately cleared, but in this case, old text should be left alone, and the cursor should be placed where it was when you left the window. You used the macro STOREXY( ) to save the cursor position. The macro GETXY( ) will use the variables *xwin* and *ywin* to restore the cursor position. It does this using the function gotoxy( ). This function will move the cursor to any *x,y* position that you specify with the parameters.

Once the cursor is in the correct position in window 1, the user is asked for cards to be drawn with the ask_then_draw( ) function. This hand is then sorted and displayed in window 2. The program then waits for a keypress.

After the user's keypress, the program displays its hand, evaluates it and reports a winner. Finally, the variables *my_score* and *his_score* are updated and the current score is displayed in window 4.

In order to run this program, you must create the files poker.c, pause.c, and chkhand.c. These files are listed along with poker.h in Figures 19-24 through 19-27.

Figure 9-24. poker.h

```
/*poker.h*/
#include <alloc.h>
#include <conio.h>
#include <stdio.h>
#define ACE 14
#define TWO 2
#define THREE 3
#define FOUR 4
#define FIVE 5
#define SIX 6
#define SEVEN 7
#define EIGHT 8
#define NINE 9
#define TEN 10
#define JACK 11
#define QUEEN 12
#define KING 13
#define SPADES 1
```

```
#define DIAMONDS 2
#define HEARTS 3
#define CLUBS 4
#define SHUFFLE_LENGTH 10000
#define TRUE -1
#define FALSE 0
#define VAL_ZIP 0
#define VAL_TWO_KIND 1
#define VAL_TWO_PAIR 2
#define VAL_THREE_KIND 3
#define VAL_STRAIGHT 4
#define VAL_FULL_HOUSE 5
#define VAL_FLUSH 6
#define VAL_FOUR_KIND 7
#define VAL_STRAIGHT_FLUSH 8
#define GETXY() gotoxy(xwin1,ywin1);
#define STOREXY() xwin1 = wherex(); ywin1 = wherey();
#define WINDOW1() window(1,16,80,25); textcolor(CYAN);
#define WINDOW2() window(1,5,40,13); textcolor(GREEN);
#define WINDOW3() window(41,5,60,13); textcolor(RED)  ;
#define WINDOW4() window(20,3,40,4); textcolor(MAGENTA);


        typedef char suit;
        typedef char rank;

        typedef struct
        {
                rank card_rank;
                suit card_suit;

        } card;

        typedef struct
        {
                rank card1,card2;
                int value;

        } card_value;

        typedef struct
        {
                rank hand_rank[5];
                suit hand_suit[5];

        } hand;
```

Figure 9-25. poker.c

```
/* poker.c */
#include "poker.h"
#define case_rank(X) case X : cprintf("%s",rank_name[X]); break;
#define case_suit(X) case X : cprintf("%s",suit_name[X]); break;

char rank_name[15][10] = {"BLANK","Blank","Two","Three","Four","Five","Six",
                          "Seven","Eight","Nine","Ten","Jack","Queen","King",
                          "Ace"};

char suit_name[5][10] = {"Blank","Spades","Diamonds","Hearts","Clubs"};

card deck[52];
int top_card=1;

void show_hand(hand *);
hand *deal_hand(void);
void init_deck(void);
void shuffle(void);
void print_value(card_value *);
card_value *eval_hand(hand *);

#include "chkhnd.c"
#include "pause.c"

void init_deck()
{
        int i,j;
        for(i=0;i<13;i++)
                for(j=0;j<4;j++)
                {
                        deck[i*4+j].card_rank=i+2;
                        deck[i*4+j].card_suit=j+1;

                }

}

void shuffle()
{

        int i;
        char card1,card2;
        card temp_card;

        top_card = 0;
        cprintf("Shuffling");
        for(i=0;i<SHUFFLE_LENGTH;i++)
        {

                if(i%1000 == 0)
                        cprintf(".");
                card1 = rand() % 52;
                card2 = rand() % 52;
                temp_card = deck[card1];
                deck[card1] = deck[card2];
                deck[card2] = temp_card;

        }
        cprintf("\n");

}

hand *draw_card(the_hand,the_card)
hand *the_hand;
int the_card;

{
        if(top_card >= 52)
        {
                cprintf("Error! No more cards!");
                return (hand *) -1;

        }
        the_hand->hand_rank[the_card] = deck[top_card].card_rank;
        the_hand->hand_suit[the_card] = deck[top_card++].card_suit;
        return the_hand;
}
```

251

```
hand *deal_hand()
{
        char ch,card;
        int i;
        hand *the_hand;

        the_hand = (hand *) malloc(sizeof(hand));

        for(i=0;i<5;i++)
                the_hand = draw_card(the_hand,i);
        return the_hand;

}

hand *ask_then_draw(the_hand)
hand *the_hand;
{

        int i;
        char tmpstr[10];
        cprintf("Draw which cards? (ex. 10101 draws 1,3,5)");
        gets(tmpstr);
        cprintf("\n\n");
        for(i=0;i<5;i++)
        {

                if(tmpstr[i] == '1')
                the_hand = draw_card(the_hand,i);
        }
        return the_hand;

}

void show_hand(the_hand)
hand *the_hand;
{

        char ch,card;
        int i;
        for(i=0;i<5;i++)
        {
            print_card(the_hand->hand_rank[i],the_hand->hand_suit[i]);
        }

}

print_card(crank,csuit)
rank crank;
suit csuit;
{
        switch(crank)
        {
                case_rank(TWO);
                case_rank(THREE);

                }
                        if(drawn !=0)
                            cprintf("I drew %d cards\n",drawn);
                        else
                            cprintf("I drew 1 card\n");
                    return the_hand;

}
  void print_val(card_val)
  card_value *card_val;
  {
        switch(card_val->value)
        {
            case VAL_FLUSH : cprintf("Flush\n");
                                        break;
            case VAL_STRAIGHT : cprintf("Straight\n");
                                        break;
            case VAL_STRAIGHT_FLUSH : if(card_val->card1 != TEN)
                                            cprintf("Straight Flush\n");
                                        else
                                            cprintf("Royal Flush\n");
                                        break;
            case VAL_FULL_HOUSE : cprintf("Full House\n");
                                        break;
            case VAL_FOUR_KIND : cprintf("Four of a Kind\n");
                                        break;
            case VAL_THREE_KIND : cprintf("Three of a Kind\n");
                                        break;
            case VAL_TWO_KIND : cprintf("Two of a Kind\n");
                                        break;
```

```
                  case VAL_TWO_PAIR : cprintf("Two pair\n");
                                              break;
                     default : cprintf("Nothing\n");
              }

        }

 main()
 {
        int i=0,his_score=0,my_score=0;
        int xwin1 = 1, ywin1 = 1;
        char ch;
        hand *my_hand,*his_hand;
              unsigned seed;

        textmode(C80);
        textcolor(LIGHTGRAY);
           clrscr();
        cprintf("\n");
        cprintf("                                    Score:\n");
        cprintf("    Your Hand");
        cprintf("--------------                                      My Hand\n");
        cprintf("\n\n\n\n\n\n\n\n\n\n----------------------------------------------------------
        init_deck();
        do
        {
                WINDOW2();
                clrscr();
                WINDOW3();
                clrscr();
                WINDOW1();
                clrscr();
                shuffle();
                cprintf("Game %d:\n",++i);
                my_hand = deal_hand();
                sort(my_hand);
                his_hand = deal_hand();

                 case_rank(FOUR);
                 case_rank(FIVE);
                 case_rank(SIX);
                 case_rank(SEVEN);
                 case_rank(EIGHT);
                 case_rank(NINE);
                 case_rank(TEN);
                 case_rank(JACK);
                 case_rank(QUEEN);
                 case_rank(KING);
                 case_rank(ACE);
                 default : cprintf("%d",crank);
            }
        cprintf(" Of ");
        switch(csuit)
        {
                case_suit(SPADES);
                case_suit(DIAMONDS);
                case_suit(HEARTS);
                case_suit(CLUBS);
                default : cprintf("%d",csuit);
        }
        cprintf("\n");
    }


 hand *pick_then_draw(the_hand)
 hand *the_hand;
 {

        card_value *card_val;
        int drawn = 0,i;

        card_val = eval_hand(the_hand);
        switch(card_val->value)
        {
                case VAL_STRAIGHT :
                case VAL_FLUSH :
                case VAL_STRAIGHT_FLUSH :
                case VAL_FULL_HOUSE :
                            break;
                case VAL_FOUR_KIND :
```

```
         case VAL_THREE_KIND :
         case VAL_TWO_KIND :
                for(i=0;i<5;i++)
                   if(the_hand->hand_rank[i] != card_val->card1)
                   {
                          drawn++;
                          the_hand = draw_card(the_hand,i);
                   )
                break;
         case VAL_TWO_PAIR :
                for(i=0;i<5;i++)
                    if(the_hand->hand_rank[i] != card_val->card1 &&
                       the_hand->hand_rank[i] != card_val->card2)
                   {

                          drawn++;
                          the_hand = draw_card(the_hand,i);
                   )
                                     break;
                   default :
                          for(i=2;i<5;i++)
                                 the_hand = draw_card(the_hand,i);
                          drawn=3;

       sort(his_hand);
       STOREXY();
       WINDOW2();
       clrscr();
       show_hand(my_hand);
       cprintf("\n");
       print_val(eval_hand(my_hand));
       WINDOW3();
       his_hand = pick_then_draw(his_hand);
       sort(his_hand);
       WINDOW1();
       GETXY();
       my_hand = ask_then_draw(my_hand);
       STOREXY();
       WINDOW2();
       clrscr();
       sort(my_hand);
       show_hand(my_hand);
       cprintf("\n");
       print_val(eval_hand(my_hand));
       WINDOW1();
       GETXY();
       pause();
       STOREXY();
       WINDOW3();
       clrscr();
       show_hand(his_hand);
       cprintf("\n");
       print_val(eval_hand(his_hand));
       WINDOW1();
       ywin1--;
       GETXY();
       textcolor(CYAN+BLINK);
       if(compare_hand(my_hand,his_hand))
       {
            my_score++;
            cprintf("You win!!                   \n");
            )
       else
       {
            his_score++;
            cprintf("I win!!                     \n");
            )

   )       STOREXY();
       WINDOW4();
       clrscr();
       cprintf("%d       to        %d\n",my_score,his_score);
       WINDOW1();
       GETXY();
       cprintf("Hit q to quit, any other key to continue.");
       ch = getch();
       )
       while(ch != 'q' && ch != 'Q');
       )
```

Figure 9-26. pause.c

```c
/* pause.c */
#include <stdio.h>

void pause()
{
                cprintf("<Hit any key to continue>\n");
                getch();
}
```

Figure 9-27. chkhnd.c

```c
/* chkhnd.c */

sort(the_hand)
hand *the_hand;
{
        int i,j;
        char temp;

        for(i=0;i<4;i++)
                for(j=i+1;j<5;j++)
                        if(the_hand->hand_rank[i]<the_hand->hand_rank[j])
                        {

                                temp = the_hand->hand_rank[j];
                                the_hand->hand_rank[j] = the_hand->hand_rank[i];
                                the_hand->hand_rank[i] = temp;
                                temp = the_hand->hand_suit[j];
                                the_hand->hand_suit[j] = the_hand->hand_suit[i];
                                the_hand->hand_suit[i] = temp;
                        }
}

straight(the_hand)
hand *the_hand;
{
        if(the_hand->hand_rank[0] == the_hand->hand_rank[1] +1 &&
           the_hand->hand_rank[1] == the_hand->hand_rank[2] +1 &&
           the_hand->hand_rank[2] == the_hand->hand_rank[3] +1 &&
           the_hand->hand_rank[3] == the_hand->hand_rank[4] +1)
                return the_hand->hand_rank[0];
        if(the_hand->hand_rank[4] == TWO && the_hand->hand_rank[0] == ACE &&
           the_hand->hand_rank[1] == the_hand->hand_rank[2] +1 &&
           the_hand->hand_rank[2] == the_hand->hand_rank[3] +1 &&
           the_hand->hand_rank[0] == the_hand->hand_rank[1] +1)
                return ACE;
        return FALSE;
}

flush(the_hand)
hand *the_hand;
{
        if(the_hand->hand_suit[0] == the_hand->hand_suit[1] &&
           the_hand->hand_suit[1] == the_hand->hand_suit[2] &&
           the_hand->hand_suit[2] == the_hand->hand_suit[3] &&
           the_hand->hand_suit[3] == the_hand->hand_suit[4])
                return TRUE;
        return FALSE;
}

four_kind(the_hand)
hand *the_hand;
{
        int i;

        for(i=0;i<2;i++)
                if(the_hand->hand_rank[i] == the_hand->hand_rank[i+1] &&
                   the_hand->hand_rank[i+1] == the_hand->hand_rank[i+2] &&
                   the_hand->hand_rank[i+2] == the_hand->hand_rank[i+3])
                        return the_hand->hand_rank[i];
        return FALSE;
}

three_kind(the_hand)
hand *the_hand;
{
        int i;
```

255

```
                for(i=0;i<3;i++)
                        if(the_hand->hand_rank[i] == the_hand->hand_rank[i+1] &&
                           the_hand->hand_rank[i+1] == the_hand->hand_rank[i+2])
                                return the_hand->hand_rank[i];
                return FALSE;
        }

        two_kind(the_hand)
        hand *the_hand;
        {
                int i;

                for(i=0;i<4;i++)
                        if(the_hand->hand_rank[i] == the_hand->hand_rank[i+1])
                                return the_hand->hand_rank[i];
                return FALSE;
        }

        two_pair(the_hand)
        hand *the_hand;
        {
                int i,j;

                for(i=0;i<2;i++)
                        if(the_hand->hand_rank[i] == the_hand->hand_rank[i+1])
                                for(j=i+2;j<4;j++)
                                        if(the_hand->hand_rank[j] == the_hand->hand_rank[j+1] &&
                                           the_hand->hand_rank[j] != the_hand->hand_rank[i])
                                                return the_hand->hand_rank[j];
                return FALSE;
        }

        full_house(the_hand)
        hand *the_hand;
        {
                int i,j;
                if(the_hand->hand_rank[0] == the_hand->hand_rank[1] &&
                   the_hand->hand_rank[2] == the_hand->hand_rank[3] &&
                   the_hand->hand_rank[3] == the_hand->hand_rank[4])
                        return the_hand->hand_rank[3];
                if(the_hand->hand_rank[0] == the_hand->hand_rank[1] &&
                   the_hand->hand_rank[1] == the_hand->hand_rank[2] &&
                   the_hand->hand_rank[3] == the_hand->hand_rank[4])
                        return the_hand->hand_rank[3];
                return FALSE;
        }

        card_value *eval_hand(the_hand)
        hand *the_hand;
        {
                card_value *card_val;

                card_val = (card_value *)malloc(sizeof(card_val));
                card_val->card1 = 1;
                card_val->card2 = 1;
                if(straight(the_hand))
                        if(flush(the_hand))
                                if(the_hand->hand_rank[0] == JACK)
                                        card_val->value = VAL_STRAIGHT_FLUSH;
                                else
                                {
                                        card_val->value = VAL_STRAIGHT_FLUSH;
                                        card_val->card1 = the_hand->hand_rank[0];
                                }
                        else
                        {
                                card_val->value = VAL_STRAIGHT;
                                card_val->card1 = the_hand->hand_rank[0];
                        }
                else
                        if(flush(the_hand))
                                card_val->value = VAL_FLUSH;
                else
                if(two_kind(the_hand))
                        if(three_kind(the_hand))
                                if(four_kind(the_hand))
                                {
                                        card_val->value = VAL_FOUR_KIND;
                                        card_val->card1 = four_kind(the_hand);
                                }
                                else
```

```
                          if(full_house(the_hand))
                          {
                                    card_val->value = VAL_FULL_HOUSE;
                                    card_val->card1 = two_kind(the_hand);
                                    card_val->card2 = full_house(the_hand);
                          }
                          else
                          {
                                    card_val->value = VAL_THREE_KIND;
                                    card_val->card1 = three_kind(the_hand);
                          }
                  else
                  if(two_pair(the_hand))
                  {
                            card_val->value = VAL_TWO_PAIR;
                            card_val->card1 = two_kind(the_hand);
                            card_val->card2 = two_pair(the_hand);
                  }
          else
          {
                  card_val->value = VAL_TWO_KIND;
                  card_val->card1 = two_kind(the_hand);
          }
  else
          card_val->value = VAL_ZIP;
  return card_val;
}

int compare_hand(hand1,hand2)
hand * hand1,* hand2;
{
        card_value *val1,*val2;
        int i;

        val1=eval_hand(hand1);
        val2=eval_hand(hand2);
        if(val1->value > val2->value)
                return TRUE;
        if(val1->value == val2->value)
        {
                if(val1->card1 > val2->card1)
                        return TRUE;
                if(val1->card1 < val2->card1)
                        return FALSE;
                if(val1->card2 > val2->card2)
                        return TRUE;
                if(val1->card2 < val2->card2)
                        return FALSE;
                for(i=0;i<5;i++)
                {
                        if(hand1->hand_rank[i]>hand2->hand_rank[i])
                                return TRUE;
                        if(hand1->hand_rank[i]<hand2->hand_rank[i])
                                return FALSE;
                }
        }
        return FALSE;
}
```

While the program is now fairly complete, there are a number of modifications that could be made. For example, you could modify it to allow for more than two players. If you were really ambitious, you could even install a betting scheme. The possibilities are endless.

Though this program is long, each section is straightforward. Programming is a building process. Sections are created one at a time. Never try to complete the program in a single effort. First, take the time to design the basic flow of the program on paper. You'll want to know some things in advance:

• What data structures will be used
• What functions will be required
• How the screen will look at each point

Once this is done, build each function individually. Work on one function at a time and don't move on until it's error-free. This way, you'll have a much easier time finding and eliminating errors. The errors are likely to occur only in the function you're currently writing.

Summary

In this chapter, for the first time, you've witnessed a program built up block by block into a complex structure.

This book left large portions of C uncovered. C is one of the most complex languages available and it is nearly impossible to cover everything in a book for beginners. With the information you've gained, you easily should be able to move on to more advanced C manuals to learn more about C.

Some of the more interesting aspects available in *Turbo C* include the ability to create "hot-key" programs such as *Side-kick* which stay in memory even after they've been run and the ability to use machine language commands directly from C. Both subjects require an in-depth knowledge of C, 8086 machine language, and the IBM personal computer. This book is a first step toward that knowledge.

Index

COMPUTE! Books

Ask your retailer for these **COMPUTE! Books** or order directly from **COMPUTE!**.

Write COMPUTE! Books, F.D.R. Station, P.O. Box 5038, New York, NY 10150.

Quantity	Title	Price*	Total
_____	COMPUTE!'s Guide to Adventure Games (67-1)	**$14.95**	_____
_____	Mapping the IBM PC and PCjr (92-2)	**$19.95**	_____
_____	COMPUTE!'s Beginner's Guide to Machine Language on the IBM PC and PCjr (83-3)	**$16.95**	_____
_____	COMPUTE!'s First Book of IBM (010-6)	**$14.95**	_____
_____	COMPUTE!'s Second Book of IBM (046-7)	**$14.95**	_____
_____	COMPUTE!'s IBM and Compatibles BASIC Program Collection (083-1)	**$17.95**	_____
_____	Using Turbo Basic (119-6)	**$16.95**	_____
_____	Turbo Pascal Handbook (37-8)	**$16.95**	_____
_____	Hard Disk Management (116-1)	**$18.95**	_____
_____	PC/MC DOS Made Easy (138-2)	**$14.95**	_____
_____	Turbo Building Blocks (126-9)	**$16.95**	_____

*Add $2.00 per book for shipping and handling.
Outside US add $5.00 air mail or $2.00 surface mail.

NC residents add 5% sales tax _____
NY residents add 8.25% sales tax _____
Shipping & handling: $2.00/book _____
Total payment _____

All orders must be prepaid (check, charge, or money order).
All payments must be in US funds.
NC residents add 5% sales tax.
NY residents add 8.25% sales tax.
☐ Payment enclosed.
Charge ☐ Visa ☐ MasterCard ☐ American Express

Acct. No._____ Exp. Date_____

Name_____

Address_____

City_____ State _____ Zip_____
*Allow 4–5 weeks for delivery.
Prices and availability subject to change.
Current catalog available upon request.